THE ROAD TO FINANCIAL FREEDOM

BARRY L. CAMERON

COLLEGE
PRESS

"I love a good road trip. And reading this book feels as though you're in the car with Barry as he drives us to the destination we all want: Financial Freedom! Get in!

Everyone wants to get to financial freedom. But few seem to know how to get there. Barry shows us the way in this intensely practical book filled with Scripture and real life illustrations.

This book is like a road map to the destination of financial freedom! You can get there!"

TIM LISTON
Lead Pastor, New Hope Church,
Manvel, TX

"Your first investment on the road to financial freedom should be to read this biblical, practical, and motivational book by my friend Barry Cameron. But don't just read it – apply it in your life, starting today! In his straightforward, no-nonsense, God-honoring approach, Barry will guide you toward financial liberation. It's a journey you'll always be thankful you took!"

LEE STROBEL
New York Times best-selling author

"This book will change everything! The biblical principles and step by step applications create an undeniable blueprint of success for anyone desiring to experience financial freedom! 'The Road to Financial Freedom,' by Pastor Barry, is the road me and my family will continue to travel!"

DARRYL STRAWBERRY
Former Major League Baseball Player,
Evangelist

"Barry Cameron is a dynamic pastor leader who will shepherd you to discover the Road to Financial Freedom. Our finances are a big part of life and the Christian faith and we are to live in blessing, not bondage. Pastor Cameron gives us solid biblical counsel and encouragement as we seek to trust and obey God with our money and possessions. I highly recommend this book!"

DR. JACK GRAHAM
Former President of the SBC
and Pastor of Prestonwood Baptist Church,
Plano, TX

"Barry Cameron has done it again! There are very few resources available that can save tens of thousands of dollars for the reader. This resource will not only give you a legacy building perspective, but very practically will save readers heaps of money with avoided future financial mistakes. There are great legacy ideas and stewardship insights in here that all ultimately point to managing well for Christ and for His glory. This is life-changing content!"

CHRIS BROWN
Pastor/Speaker,
Former Nationally Syndicated Radio Host

"In my former life, the media once called me 'the biggest money earner the mob had seen since Al Capone!' I knew how to make money, but unfortunately the way I managed it did not put me on the road to financial freedom. Quite the opposite. Today, as a follower of Jesus Christ, a husband, father and businessman I can tell you that the biblical road map my friend Barry Cameron provides, in managing your finances, will provide for your financial security, peace of mind and a much more secure and enjoyable retirement. I made changes in managing my finances even before I finished reading the book. I found the information provided that sensible.

I'm gonna make you an offer you can't afford to refuse! Read this book!"

MICHAEL FRANZESE
Former Colombo family capo,
Speaker, author, follower of Jesus Christ

"It seems that two extremes appear when it comes to money. Some teach the "prosperity gospel," promising that every Christian is guaranteed to be healthy, wealthy, and happy if they'll just have enough faith and write big checks. Others teach the "poverty gospel," insisting that Christians should be poor and that wealth is sinful. Barry Cameron has faithfully avoided these unhealthy extremes, while providing us with a balanced and practical roadmap for Christian stewardship. No matter your net worth, God calls you to manage your money in a way that honors him. This book will provide you with much needed wisdom!" **COSTI W. HINN**
Author of *God, Greed, and the (Prosperity) Gospel*

"Barry Cameron's passion to fight for people's freedom is readily apparent. This book serves as a reminder that how we manage our finances is an MRI of our hearts, and that our hearts follow our financial priorities. In it, Barry lays out a clear roadmap to financial freedom and a pathway to peace as we align ourselves with what God has to say about how to handle money."

DAVE DUMMITT
Lead Pastor, 2|42 Community Church,
Brighton, MI

"Barry Cameron's Road to Financial Freedom is full of solid biblical principles, memorable illustrations and wise practical applications. It's clear, concise, well-written and extremely helpful. Parents will find it invaluable in imparting financial wisdom to their children. I believe this book will lead many to the financial freedom they long for."

RANDY ALCORN
Author of *Heaven, Safely Home*
and *Giving is the Good Life*

"More than ever in our debt-ridden society (including the church), people need to be following what God says in His Word about stewardship.
My friend Barry Cameron shows us how we can be free from financial bondage so we can serve God better."

KEN HAM
CEO, Answers in Genesis

"The Road to Financial Freedom has a way of showing us the simple yet powerful road map of reaching our financial goals. In a world where people have lost control of their financial situation, Barry Cameron has once again brought us back to the biblical and prudent road map to secure a better way of life. This is a book to help your children and grandchildren better understand the biblical principles of money and help us educate future generations. So get ready to hit the road, navigate the on ramps and exits, adjust to the detours, experience the ride of your life and learn how God owns everything! Thank you, Barry Cameron!"

DOUG CROZIER
CEO, The Solomon Foundation,
Parker, CO

"Barry Cameron has so beautifully spelled out in his wonderfully written, biblically and, experience based, time tested newly released book, The Road to Financial Freedom. Barry knows, and if you follow these principles you too will learn the joy of being debt free! I cannot say enough about the need for this book at this time of unprecedented debt in America. The average American is only one bump in the road from financial destruction. Read the book, apply the principles and trust God and you will not only survive but thrive!"

GARY D. FRAZIER, Ph.D.
President, Discovery Missions International,
Coffeyville, Texas

"The good news is, "The Road To Financial Freedom" is a very readable book – chock full of illustrations and quotes from Barry. The truth is this book is a MUST READ for anyone who has a teenager, for students in college or early career, a great gift for young couples who are in their early years of marriage, for the thousands who struggle financially! IT IS CRUCIAL that Biblical stewardship principles are established and become a habit, and The Road To Financial Freedom is the map that gives all the necessary signs and guidance to get you on the right road! Read This Book! Read it two or three times! Discuss it with your small group, friends or mate. Apply the principles, and rejoice in God's provision and blessings as you live in faith and bask in financial freedom!"

ANDY HANSEN
Senior Relational Officer and
former President of CIY (Christ In Youth)

Published by College Press Publishing Company.
2111 N. Main Street, Suite 3, Joplin, MO 64801
800-289-3300
collegepress.com

First Printing 2020
International Standard Book Number: 978-0-89900-073-2

The Library of Congress has catalogued an earlier printing as follows:

Library of Congress Cataloging-in-Publication Data

Cameron, Barry L. (Barry Lee), 1955-
      The Road to Financial Freedom/Barry L. Cameron
      p. cm.
      Includes bibliographical references.
      ISBN 0-00000-000-0 (pbk.)
      1. Finance, Personal – Religious aspects – Christianity. I. Title.
AB124.C9876 2018
000.000 – bc62

1234567890

DEDICATION

To my grandsons, Will and Levi,

who will never know the bondage of debt

and will enjoy a lifetime of financial freedom.

TABLE OF CONTENTS

ACKNOWLEDGMENTS

Special thanks to my family at Crossroads Christian Church
for putting these principles into practice and changing
the narrative for so many forever.

Thank you, Michelle Miller and Michelle Gibson,
for helping transform my thoughts and ideas into this book
so they will impact the lives of people
everywhere until Jesus comes.

If you don't change the plan,
you don't plan to change.

BLC

INTRODUCTION

Most people aren't on the road to financial freedom. They are on the road to financial ruin and don't even know it.

The majority of people have no training on how to manage money or how things work in the marketplace. Yet, money is a major part of their lives, so not knowing what to do creates all sorts of problems.

Every time we plug something in or flip a switch, we're spending money. Every time we turn on a faucet or flush a toilet, we're spending money. Every time we turn the key in the ignition of our car, the clock starts ticking and we're spending money.

Electricity is a wonderful thing, but it's not free. It costs us money. If something beeps, blinks, buzzes, hums, glows, lights up a room, provides music, broadcasts images, helps you brush your teeth, keeps your food fresh and your milk cold, vacuums the dirt off your carpet, turns ordinary bread into toast, delivers a hot cup of coffee – it's costing you money.

Talk radio is free, but not the actual radio we're using to hear it. Whenever we plug something into an electrical socket, we're spending money. Did you ever stop to count the number of electric clocks in your home? All of them do two things: Tell us the time and cost us money.

When we open the refrigerator door, the cold air coming out feels good, but it costs money to cool the inside again once the door is closed. Making ice is a 24-hour job – again, costing money. Ceiling fans are nice, but with every turn the electric meters on the outside of our homes are turning too.

What about cell phones? They cost us money without even turning them on. Every time we turn down the air conditioning to make ourselves cooler? You guessed it – more money. Turn up the heat, same thing. Turn on the fake fireplace? Yep. More money. Gas is currently cheaper than electricity, but it still costs money.

When we get out of bed in the morning, turn on the coffee maker, plug in the toaster, and turn on the TV to watch *Good Morning America*, we're spending money and we haven't even left the house yet. Every time we leave the house, even to go to work, we're spending money. When we go out to eat or to a movie, it costs us money. Hire a babysitter or decide to skip the movie altogether and just stop for a soda or Starbucks? More money. If we stay home thinking we won't spend any money, we're still spending money because of our rent, mortgage, utilities . . . and the list goes on and on.

We're experts on spending, novices on saving, and knuckleheads when it comes to planning for our future when we're not receiving a paycheck from our current job – or any job for that matter. When we stop earning, the clock doesn't stop ticking. Just because we stop making money doesn't mean the expenses taking our money will stop or will be given to us for free.

A number of expenses continue to work against us even when we're no longer working. For example, property taxes, school taxes, homeowner association fees, utilities, gasoline, groceries, lawn care, internet, cable or satellite TV, maintenance and repairs on our vehicles, our homes, and every appliance. Not to mention our possessions age just as we do; they break down and need to be replaced. Those expenses will never end until the end.

Is there any hope for getting ahead of the game? Any way to chart a different course with a different result? Any other road besides the road to financial ruin?

Absolutely.

There's a completely different way to live with a completely different destination that will change everything in our lives. But the only way to get there is to get on the road to financial freedom.

To steal a line from poet Robert Frost, the road to financial freedom is "the one less traveled." Anyone who wants to get on the road to financial freedom can get on it, but most don't. Why? They follow what everyone else is doing, giving no thought to the fact there might be a better way.

Frost is famous for these lines: "Two roads diverged in a wood, and I – I took the one less traveled by, and that has made all the difference."

The road to financial freedom will make all the difference in the world for you, your family, and your future, if you choose it. So, what will you do?

I can show you the way.

BARRY L. CAMERON
January 2020

People who spend money
like there is no tomorrow
are always surprised when
they find out there is a tomorrow,
and now they have no money.

BLC

1

READY TO HIT THE ROAD?

Yuri Eliseev became a world junior chess champion in Russia in 2012. He attained Grandmaster status at age 17, which was unprecedented. The title *Grandmaster* is awarded by the World Chess Federation. It's the highest title a chess player can attain and once it's achieved, it's held for life. A Grandmaster is more than just a supreme chess player. Grandmasters have an uncanny ability not only to know the right moves to make, but also to anticipate all the potential moves their opponents could make, and they're able to do it with such quickness and precision they are virtually unbeatable.

Yuri was a modern-day phenomenon. He won the Moscow Open in 2016 and was ranked 42nd among Russian Grandmasters and 212th in the world. He was only 20 years old when he died in November 2016.

How did he die? Apparently, he was playing another game called parkour. The name is taken from the phrase *parcours du combattant* – the path of the warrior. It's the military obstacle course training devised by French physical educationalist Georges Hébert. It's what James Bond and the guy he was chasing were doing at the beginning of *Casino Royale* as they leaped across roofs, fences, and other man-made objects. Yuri was playing the game by trying to jump to another balcony 12 stories above the street.[1]

He missed.

When I heard that story, I wondered how someone so good at knowing all the right moves made such a bad move – such a costly one? Then I realized most of us do it all the time – with our finances.

When it comes to money, we all know what we ought to do. We even know what other people ought to do. We just don't do it, and the financial consequences can be deadly.

In the pages that follow, I'm going to provide a biblical theology (since the Bible is the ultimate and final authority for our lives and God is the owner of everything) and a practical strategy so you can get on the road to financial freedom and stay there the rest of your life. You can begin to rewrite your story and the story of everyone you know and love. It won't be easy, even though the strategy is simple, and it won't happen overnight. But by this time tomorrow night, you could already be well on your way.

So, let's get started.

In Luke 16:1-15, Jesus told the parable of the dishonest manager. In the previous chapter Luke recounted the parable of the dishonorable son (Luke 15:11-32). We know it as the story of the prodigal son. It's really the story of a son who dishonored his family and his father and squandered all of his wealth.

These back-to-back parables illustrate the *wrong* way and then the *right* way to manage the resources God gives us.

The prodigal son squandered what was given to him. But the dishonest manager shrewdly managed what he was given. This is something each of us should shoot for: being shrewd, or smart, with whatever God gives us.

Jesus told 38 parables in the Bible; 16 deal with money and how we're to manage it. Money is a vitally important subject. We deal with money every single day in one way or another.

How we get it, keep it, invest it, spend it, borrow it, manage it, give it, and get more of it so we can do it all over again. Money is important to us.

American poet Richard Armour wrote about money, "Workers earn it, spendthrifts burn it, bankers lend it, women spend it, forgers fake it, taxes take it, dying leave it, heirs receive it, thrifty save it, misers crave it, robbers seize it, rich increase it, gamblers lose it, I could use it." I'd change that last line to, "God says, 'Use it.'" God wants us to manage whatever He gives us in a way that honors Him. That's why Jesus had so much to say about money and our management of it.

Jesus talks about money, and so does the entire Bible. In the New Testament alone, there are 500 verses on prayer, 400 verses on faith, but more than 2,000 verses on money and money management – that's one out of every 10 verses in the gospels. So it's a very important subject, and what Jesus teaches in this parable may be the most important of all:

> Jesus also said to the disciples, "There was a rich man who had a manager, and charges were brought to him that this man was wasting his possessions. And he called him and said to him, 'What is this that I hear about you? Turn in the account of your management, for you can no longer be manager.' And the manager said to himself, 'What shall I do, since my master is taking the management away from me? I am not strong enough to dig, and I am ashamed to beg. I have decided what to do, so that when I am removed from management, people may receive me into their houses.' So, summoning his master's debtors one by one, he said to the first, 'How much do you owe my master?' He said, 'A hundred measures of oil.' He said to him, 'Take your bill, and sit down quickly and write fifty.' Then he said to another, 'And how much do you owe?' He said, 'A hundred

3

measures of wheat.' He said to him, 'Take your bill, and write eighty.' The master commended the dishonest manager for his shrewdness. For the sons of this world are more shrewd in dealing with their own generation than the sons of light. And I tell you, make friends for yourselves by means of unrighteous wealth, so that when it fails they may receive you into the eternal dwellings.

"One who is faithful in a very little is also faithful in much, and one who is dishonest in a very little is also dishonest in much. If then you have not been faithful in the unrighteous wealth, who will entrust to you the true riches? And if you have not been faithful in that which is another's, who will give you that which is your own? No servant can serve two masters, for either he will hate the one and love the other, or he will be devoted to the one and despise the other. You cannot serve God and money" (Luke 16:1-13).

The key to the parable is found in verse eight: "For the sons of this world are more shrewd in dealing with their own generation than the sons of light." Jesus is saying the world is much better at using money to achieve their purposes than God's people are at using God's money to achieve God's purposes. And Christians ought to be better. We ought to be the experts. We ought to be better with our money than the world ever thought about being, and we ought to use it to reach people for Christ and get them to Heaven. That's what Jesus said in verse nine: "I tell you, make friends for yourselves by means of unrighteous wealth [money], so that when it fails [or when it's gone] they may receive you into the eternal dwellings." In other words, use our wealth – whatever God gives us – to help get people into Heaven, and someday when we get to Heaven, they will say to us, "I'm here because of you."

We can learn at least five powerful principles from the parable of the shrewd manager.

WE'RE GOING TO BE HELD ACCOUNTABLE FOR WHAT WE'VE BEEN GIVEN

Verses one and two make it clear, someday we will be held accountable for what God has given us. The master called in the dishonest manager and said, "What's this I hear? You haven't been honest. You haven't been trustworthy with what I entrusted to you!"

The same thing is going to happen to us one day.

Verse one clarifies that Jesus was teaching His disciples. This was not addressed to the world. Christians are called to a different, higher standard than the world. We are not to manage our resources the way the world does.

By the way, if you're getting your financial counsel from the world, you're already in trouble.

You need God's counsel. The Bible is the best book on finances. God is the Creator of it all. If something is wrong with my watch, I go to a watch repairman who understands how the watchmaker designed it. If I have a car problem, I go to the car dealership because they have trained technicians who know how my car was designed and how it works, so they know how to fix it.

Why is it then, when it comes to so many things in our lives, too often the last place we turn is the manual – the Bible – given to us by the Creator of everything in the universe?

We're accountable to God for at least two reasons:

1. Everything belongs to Him. Psalm 24:1 says, "The earth is the Lord's, and everything in it" (*NIV*). We'll see that in more detail in the next chapter.

2. Everything comes from Him. James 1:17 says, "Every good and perfect gift is from above" (*NIV*). That means whatever we have comes from God and belongs to God. It's all His. If you think it's all yours, the day will come when you won't be able to earn any more money, get any more money, or spend any more money, and you'll finally realize it wasn't yours in the first place.

Years ago, I was with my father-in-law when his wife was dying of cancer. He turned to me and said, "Barry, I would give everything I have and every dime I have to keep my wife." Money didn't mean a thing then, and it couldn't do anything for him. Property didn't mean a thing. Cars didn't mean a thing. Rental buildings didn't mean a thing.

Don't wait until it's too late to learn that *it all belongs to God* and *it all comes from Him*. It's so much better for us to learn that lesson sooner rather than later. We need to learn it today.

So Jesus said we are not to manage our resources the way the world does. Deuteronomy 8:18 says, "But remember the Lord your God, for it is he who gives you the ability to produce wealth, and so confirms his covenant" (*NIV*). The ownership issue is one we all have to settle. And if we don't settle the ownership issue, we're going to be at odds with God about everything.

When we think it's ours but it's really His, nothing's going to work. God gives us everything we have, and we need to manage whatever He gives us in a way that honors Him. When we do, He'll give us more.

IF WE'RE NOT TRUSTWORTHY, GOD WILL GET SOMEONE ELSE TO MANAGE HIS RESOURCES

This is a big one. Jesus said the dishonest manager lost his job. He got fired. Why? Because he was dishonest.

Have you ever noticed Jesus never uses anyone's name in His parables? He never says, "Let me tell you about Bartholomew and what he did." He never says, "Let me tell you about Sandra and what she did." Why? Because this might be *your* story.

In much the same way this dishonest manager lost his job, some people have lost their jobs as managers of God's resources a long time ago, but they don't even know it. I hope that's not your story.

Why would someone lose their job as a manager of God's resources? Because God can't trust them. They are dishonest.

Like Ananias and Sapphira in Acts 5, we can fool the people around us, but we can't fool the God above us. So, rather than strike us dead like God did that couple, He finds someone else to bless, someone else to use, someone else He can trust, someone who won't be dishonest with His resources.

Someone is bound to think, *I'm getting along just fine. I've got more money now than I've ever had. Things are going great.* That may be. But you are not a manager of God's resources. You're a maintainer of your own. There's a difference. And you have no idea what you're missing because you're doing your own thing instead of doing what God says.

Don't miss this: *Unfaithfulness unplugs us from God's unlimited resources, and when something's unplugged it doesn't have any power.*

When we put ourselves first by being selfish, doing our own thing, thinking it's all about us, we're really saying, "God, I don't trust You." But even worse, we're also telling Him, "God, You can't trust me." When we come to church only when we feel like it or skip church altogether when we're out of town or on vacation, even though the Bible says we're not to give up meeting together, "as is the habit of some" (Hebrews 10:25), we're telling God, "You can't trust me."

A preacher friend once told me, "When I'm on vacation I don't go to church."

"What?" I was shocked.

"No man, on my vacation I don't even have a quiet time," he said. "I'm

7

on vacation. I'm taking a break."

"You're out of your mind," I said. And then I told him, "I have a quiet time and go to church not because I'm a pastor. I do it because I'm a Christian."

Isn't that legalism? you might ask. No. That's love for God and His Word.

When we do things like that, we're telling God we don't trust Him and we don't trust His plan. We're also telling God He can't trust us.

That idea may have never occurred to you, but it's essentially what we're saying when we do such things. When we don't tithe, even though the Bible is crystal clear on that, we're telling God we don't trust Him to provide for our needs. And we're telling Him He can't trust us.

Tony Evans said, "If people don't tithe . . . [then] you don't believe it. Don't say you believe it, but you don't do it." A person wouldn't say, "I believe in bathing, I just don't do it. . . . The fact of the matter is, if you don't do it, you don't believe it."

You need to realize you are telling God you don't trust Him, you don't trust what He says, and He can't trust you.

When we don't pray, and when we try to work things out on our own strength and power, we're saying, "God, we don't trust You to take care of our problems and our issues in life." We're also saying, "God, You can't trust me."

Do you want to know what God does with people who can't be trusted? He doesn't trust them with anything. He finds someone else who can be trusted. Many people go to church, claim to be Christians, and claim to love Jesus, but because of their dishonesty and the fact they aren't trustworthy, they've lost their job as a manager of God's resources. And they don't even know it.

WE SHOULD ALWAYS PUT PEOPLE ABOVE PERSONAL PROFIT

In Luke 16:3-7, this dishonest manager who was preparing to lose his job asked himself, *"What can I do? I can't dig and I don't want to beg."* His response reflects his shrewdness. He was smart enough to realize people are more important than personal profit, and the master commended him for that.

I want to be clear. Jesus did not commend the dishonest manager for his dishonesty, but rather, for his shrewdness in recognizing people were more important than personal profit. That shrewd manager realized friends were going to be more important than finances. In fact, when his finances were gone, he would need all the friends he could get.

Jesus also commended the shrewd manager because he took action immediately to fix the problem. We should be shrewd like that – smart enough to take advantage of the opportunities before us. In fact, we ought to be better at it than the world is.

Verse 9 is the key to the parable. Jesus said, "And I tell you, make friends for yourselves by means of unrighteous wealth [that's our money], so that when it fails [or when it is gone] they may receive you into the eternal dwellings [that's Heaven]." Jesus was saying, "Don't waste your wealth on stuff. Invest it in people. Help them get to Heaven."

Am I saying we can't ever spend money on stuff? Not at all. In fact, when I was writing this we had to buy a brand-new dishwasher. You see, the dishwashers – our kids – have all moved out.

So we had to get a machine to do it, and that machine finally broke down. Sometimes you've got to spend money on a machine. I don't like spending money on machines, but that's a reality of life.

Here's the good news: When you pay off all your debts and don't owe a bunch of money on stuff you no longer own or stuff that no longer works, or you no longer owe more on a car than it's actually worth, you get out of that rat race and it's a lot easier to buy whatever machine you need.

The Bible doesn't say we can't spend money on stuff. It says we need to do what God says. It's not that we can't spend money on a house or a car or a multitude of other things. But the reality is, the most important investment we can ever make is in the lives of people to help them get to Heaven. That's why we ought to be better managers of our money. Our house is paid off, our cars are paid off, and we don't have any debt, so when God wants us to do something, we can say, "Yes, Sir. I'll do whatever You say."

Maybe you can't say that today and instead you have to tell God, "Well, I'd love to do what You're asking me to do, but First National Bank and Kohl's and Citibank have to be paid first." Too often, we've got all these other gods we must answer to first. How in the world did that happen? Because we didn't do what God said and we have to change that.

Jesus' point is this: When all of our wealth on earth is gone, the only thing that will matter is the investment we've made in Heaven.

THE TRUST ISSUE DETERMINES OUR FUTURE

Verses 10-12 say, "One who is faithful in a very little is also faithful in much, and one who is dishonest in a very little is also dishonest in much. If then you have not been faithful in the unrighteous wealth [money], who will entrust to you the true riches? And if you have not been faithful in that which is another's, who will give you that which is your own?"

If we can't be trusted in the little things, God is not going to give us more. Our faithfulness with what God has already given us determines what He will give us in the future. And if we can't be trusted, He'll find someone else who can be.

Solomon said, "Of what use is money in the hand of a fool, since he has no desire to get wisdom?" (Proverbs 17:16, *NIV* 1984). God is saying, "Why in the world would I give you any more money when you've been acting like a fool with what I've already given you?"

God's not going to ignore our foolishness and mismanagement of what He's given us and then give us more. You don't want to live your life in a way that says, *God, I don't trust You and I don't trust Your plan.* You don't want to live your life in a way that says, *God, You can't trust me. Find somebody else.* That's not how you get on the road to financial freedom. That's how you wind up in a ditch called financial collapse.

The Bible says, "Moreover, it is required of stewards [managers] that they be found faithful" (1 Corinthians 4:2). That's it. *Be faithful.*

If an employer hires a new employee and that employee is faithful, that covers everything. That employee will come to work on time. They'll do the job they're supposed to do. They'll work with the rest of the employees. They'll help the company succeed and make a profit. They'll always have the best interests of the company at heart. All of those good employee traits result from one thing: *being faithful.*

In marriage, if both people standing at the altar say "I do" and remain faithful to one another, that covers everything.

The Bible says there is one requirement of managers, of stewards – *be faithful.*

WE HAVE TO CHOOSE THE ONE WE'RE GOING TO SERVE

Jesus said, "No servant can serve two masters, for either he will hate the one and love the other, or he will be devoted to the one and despise the other. You cannot serve God and money" (Luke 16:13). We have a choice: It's God's kingdom or ours.

The world says, "Serve us. Do things our way. Follow our example." The world says, "Here are the rules. Get all you can. Can all you get. Sit on the lid. Poison the rest." The world says, "He who dies with the most toys, wins." But read the fine print. He who dies with the most toys still dies.

Then what?

Jesus said no servant can serve two masters. You cannot serve God and money. You must choose between your kingdom and God's. It can't and won't be both.

Jesus said, "Seek first the kingdom of God and his righteousness, and all these things will be added to you" (Matthew 6:33). All you need to do is make God and His kingdom the number one priority in your life and all these other things will take care of themselves.

There's a postscript to this parable in Luke 16:14-15. Luke tells us the Pharisees, who were lovers of money, heard all of these things. (Never mind that Jesus wasn't talking to the Pharisees; He was talking to His disciples.) And when the Pharisees heard all these things, they ridiculed Jesus. Some Bible translations say they sneered at Him.

So Jesus rebuked them.

Sometimes you don't say anything to critics. Sometimes you do. This time Jesus did. People who love money will always mock, ridicule, make fun of, or ignore what God says. So if you're around somebody who says, "I don't need that stuff" or "I don't follow God's plan" or "I don't tithe," you're listening to a fool. You're listening to someone who is a lover of money.

In verse 15, Jesus lays them out. He said, "You are those who justify yourselves before men, but God knows your hearts. For what is exalted among men is an abomination in the sight of God."

Have you ever noticed how people who don't follow what God says always have a rationalization for it? They justify themselves.

When it comes to serving, they'll say, "Well, I'm so busy at work, I just don't have time to serve. It's not that I don't want to serve. I used to serve years ago." Or when it comes to praying, they'll say, "I just don't feel comfortable praying in public," or, "I fall asleep when I pray at home. That's why I don't pray."

12

Are you a justifier when it comes to tithing? "I can't afford to tithe right now," you say. "I've got too many bills." The reason you have financial problems is because you haven't been following God's principles.

Several years ago, I wrote a book called *The ABCs of Financial Freedom* that told the story of our family. One of the things I included in that book was this: Financial problems are God's way of trying to get our attention to tell us something's wrong.

If you're having financial problems, stop running into a wall. The reason it's not working is because you're doing something wrong.

Are you a justifier when it comes to giving sacrificially? "I'd give more, but times are tough right now."

Jesus rebuked the justifiers because theirs was an issue of the heart. The bottom line with justifiers is they can't be trusted.

Jesus told another penetrating parable in Matthew 25. We'll look at it in more detail later. It's called the parable of the talents. When Jesus spoke of talents, He was not referring to the talent to sing, draw, write, or make animals out of balloons. The talent He referred to was a measurement of weight that was always related to money. So a talent of gold was way more valuable than a talent of silver, and a talent of silver was more valuable than a talent of bronze.

In Matthew 25:18, Jesus used the word *money*. He talked about the money that was given to this one man. I always wondered, *Why did this guy only get one talent?* I finally figured it out. That's all he could be trusted with. God measures trust not by our good intentions, but by what we're doing right now.

Jesus made a final statement in Luke 16:15: "For what is exalted among men is an abomination in the sight of God." We all know people who exalt the wrong things. They know the price of everything and the value of nothing. They're geniuses in many things, but what they exalt is an abomination in the eyes of God. Jesus couldn't have made that any clearer. When we exalt the things of men above the things of God, we've made an eternal mistake.

So we need to get our priorities right. And like the shrewd manager, who moved immediately to fix the problem, we need to move immediately to fix this problem in our lives.

Here's something else to consider: *If you don't change the plan, you don't plan to change.*

I want to change the plan of every person who reads this book. I want to change the way you think, change the way you manage, change the way you dream, and change the way you live.

Here's the bottom line to this book: If you want to get on the road to financial freedom and stay there the rest of your life, you must decide to *honor the Lord.*

It begins by honoring Him. We want God to know we trust Him and we want Him to know He can trust us.

Lord, we're going to honor You, and we're going to get on the road to financial freedom, and we're going to stay there the rest of our lives!

I want to take as many people as I can with me. I hope you'll be one of them.

- Drive carefully – biblically.

- The world is much better at using money to achieve their purposes than God's people are at using God's money to achieve God's purposes.

- We're going to be held accountable for what we've been given.

- Everything belongs to God (Psalm 24:1).

- Everything comes from Him (James 1:17).

- If we can't be trusted, God will get someone else to manage His resources.

- We should always put people above personal profit.

- If we can't be trusted in the little things, God won't give us more.

- We have to choose the master we're going to serve.

- We need to change the plan.

Manage your money when you are young
or it will manage you when you are old,
and you won't like how little there is
and what little it says you can do.

BLC

2

WHOSE ROAD IS IT ANYWAY?

Most people today have no idea what it's like to be lost. Thanks to smartphone technology, we can find any address anytime and access detailed directions on how to get somewhere . . . anywhere.

Google Maps was launched February 8, 2005. Apple devices used Google Maps initially, but Apple switched to its own mapping system in September 2012 with the release of iOS 6. That means if I type any place or address, my iPhone will find it and provide directions, and a voice will tell me, "Turn right on Debbie Lane." My iPhone can take me right to the place.

But it hasn't always been like that.

Several years ago, my wife, Janis, and I went to Orlando, Florida, for a pastor's conference. When the conference ended, we left in plenty of time to get to the airport. I've always heard you should allow extra time if you're flying out of an international airport. So we left early for Orlando International Airport and were right in front of it, when I missed my exit.

"Wasn't that the exit we were supposed to take?" Janis asked. I replied with a lame explanation that we were all right.

I kept driving and thinking there would be another exit we could take, but we kept getting farther and farther from the airport. My thinking grew more desperate: *There's got to be another entrance to this airport!* I even said to Janis, "This is the reason we come to the airport early." (Actually, that's not why we went to the airport early – so we could drive around for two hours . . . lost.)

We drove through a number of subdivisions, saw an endless number of fields and phone lines. I even drove into a cul-de-sac and had to turn around. (Did I admit yet I was completely lost?)

After almost 45 minutes we entered the far side of the airport, had to drive all the way back through it, and then made a U-turn to get to our terminal.

So what's the moral to the story besides the fact men don't like to admit they're wrong and don't like to ask for directions? Here it is: *We know when we're missing it.*

We usually know when we're not doing what we're supposed to be doing. I knew it immediately. So did my wife. Wives, when your husband isn't doing what's right, don't go along for the ride. That's not meant to be humorous. I'm serious. If my wife had said, "Barry, you missed the exit; turn around right now," what do you think I would have done?

On a Thursday, sometime after the airport adventure, we had an all-staff meeting at the church where I serve and I shared that story. I hadn't been feeling well, and Janis had been telling me I should go to the local urgent care clinic. I had been battling a pretty serious upper respiratory illness. She told me on Monday to go . . . and then on Tuesday . . . and on Wednesday. But I didn't go. After I shared that story of being lost near the airport and Janis not telling me to turn around, do you know what she said when I sat down? She said, "You're going to Care Now! Today!"

Guess who went to Care Now that afternoon? Guess who got a double steroid shot and strong antibiotics? And guess who started feeling better almost immediately?

I know some husbands who are not following God's plan and have wives who think it's their place to keep their mouths shut and just go along for the ride. But that's not how it should work. Wives, you need to speak up. You need to tell your husbands to get with the program.

Husbands, you need to love your wives enough to give them the freedom and permission to do what God says is right. We know when we're missing it and we need to listen to our wives.

There's a reason God said, "I will make a helper fit for him" (Genesis 2:18). If you're a guy, you know if not for your wife, you'd be having one fit after another. God gave you your wife. So listen to her.

Here's another nugget of wisdom: *If we don't follow the plan, we're going to feel the pain.*

That's what it's like to be lost. In simplest terms, it's painful. The people who designed, developed, and built the roads around the Orlando International Airport provided clear directions. All I had to do was *follow them.* All I had to do was go where they said to go.

Ever notice how life is so much simpler when we follow directions? And how important it is to be on the right road?

GOD OWNS THE ROAD

Psalm 24 talks about the right road and who owns it. "The earth is the Lord's and the fullness thereof, the world and those who dwell therein, for he has founded it upon the seas and established it upon the rivers" (vv. 1-2). David said everything in the world belongs to the Lord. That's the way He set it up.

Psalm 104 is a much longer psalm and goes into more detail about how everything belongs to God. It's His road.

One of the most visible yet completely ignored signs on most roads is the yield sign. I'm convinced most people in Texas have no idea what it means.

A yield sign means someone else is supposed to go first.

When it comes to the road to financial freedom, if we refuse to yield to God when it comes to money matters, it's just a matter of time before we end up wrecking our finances, our family, and our future.

Maybe you're in that position now. If so, it resulted from being unwilling to yield to God and do things His way.

Jesus said, "Seek first [God's] kingdom and his righteousness, and all these things will be given to you as well" (Matthew 6:33, *NIV*). It's very clear. Solomon said, "Honor the Lord with your wealth, with the firstfruits of all your crops; then your barns will be filled to overflowing, and your vats will brim over with new wine" (Proverbs 3:9-10, *NIV*). It's not the other way around. It's not, "When my barns are overflowing and my vats are full, then I'll honor the Lord." No. We *honor the Lord* from day one. That's where it all begins.

Pastor and author Adrian Rogers said, "We may have 'In God We Trust' on our money, but we have 'Me First' on our hearts."

Even though we know God owns the road, we can still have a hard time yielding to His direction for our lives. But – and this is a big *but* – if we don't follow God's directions, when we crash or trash our family, our finances, and our future, we can't call it an "accident." We deliberately chose not to do what God says.

How dumb is that? It's as dumb as me driving by the main entrance to Orlando International Airport and continuing to drive as if I knew where I was going, when clearly I didn't. Now that's dumb!

GOD MAKES THE RULES FOR THE ROAD

Deuteronomy 8:18 says, "Remember the Lord your God, for it is he who gives you the ability to produce wealth, and so confirms his covenant, which he swore to your ancestors, as it is today" (*NIV*).

God's in charge, not us.

Psalm 2:2-3 says, "The kings of the earth rise up and the rulers band together against the Lord and against his anointed, saying, 'Let us break their chains and throw off their shackles'" (*NIV*).

The rulers of the world say, "We don't need God. Let's get rid of Him." And the One enthroned in Heaven laughs. The Lord scoffs at them. Then He rebukes them in His anger and terrifies them in His wrath. In other words, God's in Heaven saying, "You really think you're going to be able to do it your way?"

The psalmist answers in verses 10-12: "Therefore, you kings, be wise; be warned, you rulers of the earth. Serve the Lord with fear and celebrate his rule with trembling. Kiss his son, or he will be angry and your way will lead to your destruction, for his wrath can flare up in a moment. Blessed are all who take refuge in him" (*NIV*).

The psalmist tells the rulers of the earth that if they're smart they'll love God and love His Son and do what He says. And if they'll stick close to Him, they will receive His blessings.

Another of Jesus' powerful parables tells the story of a rich fool (Luke 12:16-21). The man looked at all he had: full barns and massive amounts of land. He had so much he didn't know what to do with it all. So he said, "I'm just going to build bigger barns, and I'm going to get more storage, and I'm going to plant more crops, and I'm going to have more parties, and I'm going to make all these improvements." And God said to him, "You fool! You're out of here tonight. Now who's going to deal with all the stuff you have?"

Then Jesus added the clincher: "This is how it will be with whoever . . . is not rich toward God" (v. 21, *NIV*).

That means you might get to the place where you think it's all about you. You are set for life and you're going to enjoy it all. You've got all these plans and then something unexpected will happen. You'll get a phone call, a pink slip, a knock at the door or a word from your doctor and all of a sudden you'll

21

realize you've been a fool.

The point of the story of the rich fool is, *don't mess around.* The man in the parable was a rich fool, but he very well could have been a poor fool. A person – rich or poor – is a fool if they try to live their life and manage their finances without God. Why? Because *God owns the road and makes the rules for the road.*

GOD'S WORD CONTAINS THE RULES FOR THE ROAD

Whenever we hear someone say, "I don't know what God wants me to do," it tells us a couple of things:

1. They probably haven't been reading the Word of God and aren't regularly hearing the preaching and teaching of the Word of God. If they were, they would know a lot of what God wants them to do.

2. They don't have a personal relationship with God. If they did, they would know Him and have at least some idea of what He wants them to do.

God doesn't play some cosmic game of hide-and-seek with us. He doesn't say, "See if you can catch me."

No, God lays it out in clear, simple terms.

In John 6, Jesus explained the cost of being a disciple. And the Bible says the entire crowd left. All of them except His disciples. He turned to them and said, "Are you guys going to leave too?" Peter responded by saying, "Lord, to whom shall we go? You have the words of eternal life" (v. 68, *NIV*).

Peter got things wrong many times. But that time he got it right.

If we know the Word of God is the source of all truth, wisdom, and life, why would we ever look anywhere else?

Do you know what the Word of God can do for us? Read Proverbs 1. In the first seven verses, Solomon, the wisest man outside of Jesus Christ who ever lived, starts listing all the things the Bible can do for us. Here are a few:

It can help us attain wisdom.

It can help give us discipline.

It can help us understand words of insight.

It can help us acquire a disciplined and prudent life.

It can help us do what is right and just and fair.

It can provide us with knowledge.

It can help us have discretion.

It can give us guidance.

It can give us understanding.

Solomon said in verse 7, "The fear of the Lord is the beginning of knowledge." When we understand God is the only One we need to be concerned about, we really start to learn. Solomon added, "But fools despise wisdom and discipline" (*NIV* 1984). Fools say they don't need the Bible. They say they don't need that verse, that word from God.

In 2 Timothy 3:16-17, Paul said, "All Scripture is God-breathed and is useful for teaching, rebuking, correcting and training in righteousness, so that the servant of God may be thoroughly equipped for every good work" (*NIV*). The Bible can give us everything we need for whatever we want to do.

Peter said, "His divine power has given us everything we need for a godly life through our knowledge of him who called us by his own glory and goodness" (2 Peter 1:3, *NIV*).

The Bible can do amazing things for us. But a lot of people take their Bible, read Matthew 6:33, "Seek first the kingdom of God and his righteousness, and all these things will be added to you," and decide, "I don't want to do that. I'm not going to do that. I'm just going to rip that out of my Bible."

Or they read Proverbs 3:9-10: "Honor the Lord with your wealth, with the firstfruits of all your crops" (*NIV*). Then they say, "Firstfruits? I'm not going to give that to God. I'm going to tear that page out of my Bible."

Or how about the verse that says, "Bring the whole tithe into the storehouse, that there may be food in my house" (Malachi 3:10, *NIV*)? They read that and say, "I'm not going to tithe. I don't need to do that."

Some people would never literally tear a page from a Bible, but that's essentially what they're doing when they attempt to live their lives apart from it.

One particular verse rocked my world with regard to finances. It is one small example of why we need to listen to and follow God's Word.

It's 1 Timothy 6:7: "For we brought nothing into the world, and we cannot take anything out of the world." That one verse provides vital perspective about money and finances and offers insights into our management of them.

We didn't bring anything "in" with us. We're not taking anything "out" with us. So none of what we have is "ours." It belongs to God. Everything is His and we better *follow His plan* for managing it while we're here.

GOD OWNS THE ROAD TO FINANCIAL FREEDOM
AND MAKES THE RULES FOR THE ROAD

Here are some of the rules for the road to financial freedom:

Rule 1: Everything belongs to God. "The earth is the Lord's and the fullness thereof, the world and those who dwell therein" (Psalm 24:1). It all belongs to Him.

Rule 2: Everything we have comes from God, even what we give back to Him. We can sometimes feel pride when we give something to God. We write a big check, make a big donation, give a large online gift, or sell a piece of property and decide to give 10 percent of the proceeds to God. We get excited about what *we're* giving to God. But in reality, the only thing we're giving to God is what He gave us first. We're not really giving Him anything. We're not giving to Him from *our* stuff or *our* stash. He gave it to us in the first place.

David nailed it when he said, "But who am I, and who are my people, that we should be able to give as generously as this? Everything comes from you [God], and we have given you only what comes from your hand" (1 Chronicles 29:14, *NIV*).

I don't want to discourage or disappoint you, but the fact is we don't ever give a thing to God that He didn't give to us first. So it's foolish of us to act high and mighty and spiritual and generous when we decide to give something back to God that He gave us in the first place.

Rule 3: We are managers, not owners, and we have one job: *be faithful*. The Bible says, "Moreover, it is required of stewards that they be found faithful" (1 Corinthians 4:2).

How are you doing so far?

Rule 4: A tithe of everything we receive belongs to the Lord. That's what the Bible says. "A tithe of everything from the land, whether grain from the soil or fruit from the trees, belongs to the Lord; it is holy to the Lord" (Leviticus 27:30, *NIV*). Regardless of where our income originates, 10 percent belongs to God. Sometimes people say to me, "I don't tithe my money, I tithe my time." I respond, "Good. A tithe of *everything* you have belongs to the Lord. That's where it all begins."

Larry Burkett was the first Christian financial expert I ever knew. His simple, biblical approach to finances and money management changed my life.

Burkett was in a Bible study with other Christian businessmen and they started asking questions about money and money management.

They wondered if the Bible said anything about those subjects. So Burkett started looking up Scripture passages. He wasn't a Bible scholar or a Bible-college graduate. He just started looking up verses and then shared them with these guys.

The lives of those Christian businessmen changed as they followed God's principles. The Bible study grew into what eventually became Crown Financial Ministries, which now operates internationally. Burkett ended up writing more than 70 books, most of them about finances. He died in 2003 after a long battle with cancer.

Burkett used to talk about his wealth-building strategy, a plan where anybody could build incredible wealth and be a blessing to God at the same time. He called it the 10/10/80 plan: give 10 percent to God, give 10 percent to yourself (deposit it into your savings), and live on 80 percent.

If you set aside for a moment what the Bible says about tithing (don't set it aside for very long though), from a purely mathematical perspective, from a financial planner's perspective, that's genius. Give 10 percent to God, put 10 percent in savings, and live on 80 percent. It's brilliant.

Imagine if every one of us had saved 10 percent of every paycheck we'd received during our lifetimes. I'm sure, had we done this, every one of us would be better off than we are now. Way better off.

Do you know what's even greater than the 10 percent each of us would now have? It's the 10 percent we would have given to God. Because He's the One who owns it all and determines everything we have. When we give the first 10 percent of whatever He gives us back to Him, the Bible says He "opens the floodgates of blessing and pours out so much blessing we won't have room enough for it!" Bringing 10 percent (known as tithing) is how we plug into God's supernatural blessings. I'll discuss tithing more in subsequent chapters and answer your questions about it in Chapter 5.

Begin with the 10/10/80 plan. It's a great place to start. As you grow, and as God blesses you, you can adjust those percentages to where you are giving more, saving more, and spending less.

Rule 5: God expects a return on His investment. God expects a return on His investments, just like we do. Jesus illustrated that powerfully in the parable of the talents in Matthew 25:14-30. One man was given five talents. Another was given two. The third was given one.

The man who was given five talents doubled them and they became ten. The man given two talents doubled his as well and they became four. The third man was given one talent and he hid it. He hoarded it. He buried it in the ground. The master said the one talent given to him was to be taken away and given to the man with ten talents. Then the one-talent man was called a wicked, lazy servant, and was punished. And the punishment was severe. In the story Jesus told, the master said, "Cast the worthless servant into the outer darkness . . . [where] there will be weeping and gnashing of teeth" (v. 30).

Jesus was telling the story about the management of the resources given by the "master" – God. And where does the one who does not rightly manage his resources end up? "Outer darkness" where there will be "weeping and gnashing of teeth." That's serious. Eternally serious.

Maybe it's time we started paying more attention to what God says about how we manage His resources. How we manage them is serious to God.

Rule 6: God expects us to work. It doesn't matter who we are, where we're from, who we know, or what we've done – God expects us to work. I know it's worse than cursing in our current culture to suggest that everyone ought to have a job. We live in a culture in which millions of people think the government and everybody else ought to give them something. These folks don't believe they should have to work for it. They shouldn't have to ask for it or do anything for it.

That's not what the Bible teaches. In fact – and this may shock you – according to the Bible, our government is not supposed to give us anything. Someone may say, "Well, we pay taxes." That's right. And Romans 13 says we need to submit to the governing authorities in our lives. Our taxes help provide for an organized civilization with roads, streets, streetlights, police officers, firefighters, and certain other things. But beyond those basic services, they're not supposed to give us anything.

A lot of people will be offended by that statement because they love government programs, government handouts, and various other freebies, which really aren't free, because someone has to pay for them. In case you think all government giveaways are good, understand this: In order for the government to give freebies to people who refuse to work, they have to take money from those who do work.

Paul wrote, "For even when we were with you, we would give you this command: If anyone is not willing to work, let him not eat. For we hear that some among you walk in idleness, not busy at work, but busybodies" (2 Thessalonians 3:10-11).

Some parents let their twentysomething college students move back home.

"How old is your boy?"

"He's 24."

"Does he have a job?"

"No, he had a job and lost it."

"What does he do?"

"He likes to play video games and he's on his iPad a lot."

"Is he looking for a job?"

"Yeah, he says he is."

I'd tell those parents, "Go home today and put a padlock on the refrigerator. Don't feed him a dog biscuit or let him sip a brand-new bottle of water until he gets a job. He needs to work."

When are we going to wake up? We've produced a generation addicted to entitlements, so today we have millions of people with no desire to work;

they want everything given to them.

They're not interested in a hand up. They want a handout. They're not interested in work. They want welfare. They're not interested in what God has to say. They want to see what the government has to give.

And it's all wrong.

We'll get into this in more detail in the next chapter. I'm going to show you where the source of all this nonsense comes from.

Did you ever hear somebody say, "Those chickens are going to come home to roost"? It all begins at home.

It's a different situation when people are physically unable to work, of course. We are supposed to help them. But that's not the biggest issue in our country or our world. Our biggest issue is that so many people have been raised to believe somebody else owes them something.

Nobody owes anybody anything. We need to do what God says: Get a job. Go to work.

Rule 7: God expects us to be generous givers. We are expected to be generous givers. We are not to be tightwad tippers. The Bible says, "The point is this: whoever sows sparingly will also reap sparingly, and whoever sows bountifully will also reap bountifully" (2 Corinthians 9:6).

Richard Halverson said, "Jesus Christ said more about money than any other single thing because, when it comes to a man's real nature, money is of first importance. Money is an exact index to a man's true character. All through Scripture there is an intimate correlation between the development of a man's character and how he handles his money."[2]

For example, Jesus said, "It is more blessed to give than to receive" (Acts 20:35). But the majority of our world doesn't believe that and doesn't live that way.

The greater blessings always come to those who've learned to be

29

generous. Solomon said, "One man gives freely, yet gains even more; another withholds unduly, but comes to poverty" (Proverbs 11:24, *NIV*).

If you're generous and give, you're not going to run out of money. You're going to run out of time. God has promised that if you learn to give, "you will be enriched in every way so that you can be generous on every occasion" (2 Corinthians 9:11, *NIV*).

Rule 8: We are to use the wealth God gives us to reach people for Him. We saw this in Chapter 1. Jesus said, "I tell you, use worldly wealth to gain friends for yourselves, so that when it is gone, you will be welcomed into eternal dwellings" (Luke 16:9, *NIV*).

Tony Evans said, "Any discussion of economics that does not include God is a travesty because he is the Author of all wealth. God owns it all . . . Communism teaches that the government owns everything. Capitalism teaches that the individual owns everything. Christianity teaches that God owns everything."[3]

So whose road is it? God's. The next question is, are we going to follow His directions and follow *His rules for the road*?

Remember 1 Timothy 6:7: "For we brought nothing into the world, and we cannot take anything out of the world."

If you want to get on the road to financial freedom and stay there the rest of your life, it begins by getting to the place where you decide you're going to *honor the Lord* and *follow His plan*.

- We need to follow God's directions.

- God makes the rules.

- God's Word contains the rules.

- We are managers, not owners, and we have one job: be faithful.

- A tithe (10%) of everything we receive belongs to the Lord.

- God expects a return on His investment.

- God expects us to work.

- God expects us to be generous givers.

- We are to use the wealth God gives us to reach people for Him.

DID YOU KNOW...
"The first factory-installed seat belts happened in 1950.
The first 3-point safety belt was patented in 1958.
But it wasn't until 1984 that New York became the
first state to mandate drivers use a seat belt."

(Source : https://saferide4kids.com/blog/history-of-seat-belts-effective/)

If you always spend more than you make,
you'll never make enough.

BLC

3

ON-RAMPS AND EXITS

The most-visited museum in all of Scandinavia is in Stockholm, Sweden. It contains the world's only preserved 17th-century ship – a Swedish warship built between 1626 and 1628 during the reign of King Gustavus Adolfus, who is considered one of the great military minds in European history.

The *Vasa*, built on the king's orders as part of a military expansion during a war with Poland-Lithuania, was constructed from the timber of 1,000 oak trees; it had two gun decks with 64 bronze cannons and a mast that was more than 150 feet tall. The ship was covered with sculptures carved from oak and pine or linden. Nearly 500 of these sculptures were strategically positioned all over the ship to glorify the genius and power of the king, but also to terrify, taunt, and intimidate the enemy.

When the ship was finished, it was one of the most powerfully armed vessels in the world. However, on August 10, 1628, barely 1,400 yards into its maiden voyage, the ship sank while a crowd of hundreds, if not thousands, of Stockholmers watched in horror on the shore.[4]

Why did this magnificent, massive warship sink? The designers had put everything imaginable into and onto that great ship, but they forgot the single most important thing: A ship must float. Today, millions of people from all over the world come to see the remains of a ship that didn't do what it was supposed to do. Its designers, craftsmen, and builders worked hard and were precise in their construction and attention to every detail except one: The boat must float.

Our culture has capsized and our world has sunk to the depths of depravity, as well. Because we've forgotten what a family is supposed to do. In the rest of this chapter, I'll give you some vital reminders from God's Word.

HONOR THE LORD

We love the first three verses of Ephesians 6 because they deal with our kids: "Children, obey your parents in the Lord, for this is right. 'Honor your father and mother' (this is the first commandment with a promise), 'that it may go well with you and that you may live long in the land.'"

Those verses are great, but then we skip over verse 4: "Fathers, do not provoke your children to anger, but bring them up in the discipline and instruction of the Lord."

The home is supposed to be the greatest on-ramp for life. Unfortunately, for many it has become a fatal exit from which most people never recover. If we don't learn the right principles at home, where can we learn them? Surely no parent wants to make life harder and more difficult for their kids.

God designed the home to consist of one man and one woman – one father, one mother. (See Genesis 2:18-24.) Together they are to give birth to, provide for, protect, and prepare their kids for life. I'm sure some will say we don't have homes like that anymore.

That's my point.

The word used for *fathers* in Ephesians 6 usually refers to male parents. But it was sometimes used of parents in general. Paul was speaking about both parents, moms and dads, in the first three verses, and it's very likely he still was speaking to both parents in verse 4. So the verse could be translated this way: "*Parents,* do not provoke your children to anger, but bring them up in the training and instruction of the Lord."

How do parents provoke their children to anger? This may surprise you. The number one way is by not doing what a parent is supposed to do – not being a father, not being a mother. God places married couples in a home and gives them the blessing of children so they can raise their children in the discipline and instruction of the Lord. God expects parents to teach their children what God wants them to know. But trouble begins when a parent decides, *I'm not going to be a father* or *I'm not going to be a mother.* Turn on almost any news program any night of the week and you'll find someone talking about the problems of crime, gun violence, unwed pregnancies, gangs, drugs, alcohol abuse, and the people who are in prison. If they interview the people involved, it almost always goes back to, "I didn't have a good home life. I didn't have a father. I didn't have a mom."

That's the number one way we provoke our kids to anger – by not doing what we're supposed to do.

The second way parents provoke their kids to anger is by saying one thing and doing another – in other words, having two sets of rules or two different ways of doing things. Actions do speak louder than words. And you can sum it up with one word – *hypocrisy.* No parent wants to be called a *hypocrite,* but when we call ourselves *Christians* and don't raise our children the way God says to do it, that's what we are: *hypocrites.*

I remember being a child riding in the back seat of a car driven by one of our neighbors who went to our church. I had great respect for him until he lit up a cigarette. I remember it like it was yesterday. I said, "Mr. Wilson [not his real name], you shouldn't be smoking." He looked back at me and said, "You do as I say, not as I do."

I knew that was wrong and lost respect for him that day. Why? Because there were two sets of rules. Parents need to know that having two sets of rules frustrates their kids and provokes them. Don't provoke your children to anger, but bring them up in the discipline and instruction of the Lord.

What should parents be teaching their kids?

Author and pastor John MacArthur says, "The key to right discipline and instruction of children is its being of the Lord. Everything parents do for their children is to be of Him – according to the teaching of His Word, by the guidance and power of His Holy Spirit, in the name of His Son, Jesus Christ, and to His own glory and honor."[5]

Home is where we're supposed to learn about living. Home is where we're supposed to learn about learning. Home is where we're supposed to learn about helping and serving. Home is where we're supposed to learn about loving and giving and working and so much more.

Home is where young boys ought to be taught to become young men – godly men. Home is where young girls ought to be taught to become young women – godly women. No one is supposed to grow up godless or become godless.

Every problem of sexual identity and all the gender confusion we see in our world today started in homes where, instead of being fabulous on-ramps for life, they became fatal exits.

In this case, home is where the problem is. Homes where dads and moms abdicated their God-given roles and responsibilities for something else, or someone else, and forgot little ones were watching and waiting for someone – anyone – to show them what they were supposed to do.

Susanna Wesley, the mother of John and Charles Wesley, two of the greatest preachers who ever lived, raised 17 children. She said this about raising kids: "The parent who studies to subdue [self-will] in his child works together with God in the renewing and saving of a soul. The parent who indulges it does the devil's work, makes religion impracticable, salvation unattainable, and does all that in him lies to damn his child, soul and body forever."[6]

We can sum up what she said this way: You can either partner with God or you can partner with the devil. Just know the results will be eternal.

Several years ago, we were in Nassau, the capital city of the Bahamas. We were staying on Paradise Island and had rented some Jet Skis to go out on the water and have some fun with another family from our church. My youngest daughter, Kelli, who was in the seventh grade at the time, was going to ride with me.

I paid the rental fee, got our life vests, listened to some instructions, and headed out onto the ocean. The water was rough as we navigated the incoming waves, but I got the hang of it and we were heading farther and farther from shore. But the waves and choppiness never let up, even though I tried to make it as smooth as possible.

Kelli asked, "Dad, we're OK out here, right?" That's all she had to say. I was already having second thoughts about what we were doing. I was in water I had never been in, had no idea how deep it was or what else was in there with us, and didn't know what I would do if something went wrong. In that moment, I instantly knew my role and responsibility as a father. I needed to take care of my daughter and make sure she was safe.

I told her I didn't like the rough waves either and was going to head back in. She instantly agreed with me. To this day, I have never regretted that decision or making it as quickly as I did. It was my job as a father.

Parents, our kids want to know we're doing what's right and what's best for them at all times. They deserve to know that. They want to know we've got this. They want to know they can trust us, and follow us, and that they'll end up great.

We need to take our responsibility seriously for two primary reasons. One, because of who is counting on us – our kids. And two, because of who is holding us responsible – God. "Fathers [parents], do not provoke your children to anger, but bring them up in the discipline and instruction of the

Lord" (Ephesians 6:4).

All parents ought to want their children to succeed. If not, they shouldn't have kids. Who wants their kids to grow up and be colossal failures in life? All parents should want to start their children on the road to financial freedom. Why would you want or allow your kids to get on the road to financial collapse when you could have made things different?

All parents should make sure their children learn and live by the principles and practices that will lead them to financial freedom. They ought to say to their kids, "Follow us, and we'll show you how to do this. You'll end up great!"

If we want to get on the road to financial freedom and stay there for the rest of our lives, we need to *honor the Lord.* That's where it all begins. If we start there, everything else is going to work. If we don't start there, it won't matter what else we do.

FOLLOW GOD'S PLAN

Second, we need to *follow God's plan.* In Luke 16:8-9, Jesus said we ought to be better with our money than the world is and ought to use our money to reach people for Him and help them get to Heaven. God will meet our needs, and even some of our wants every once in a while, as long as we are using whatever He gives us to ultimately help people get to Heaven.

We also need to follow all the directions He gives in His Word. Not just the ones we like, not just the easy ones – all of them. And we need to teach our kids how to do that, which means we must be doing it first.

Solomon said, "Honor the Lord with your wealth and with the firstfruits of all your produce; then your barns will be filled with plenty, and your vats will be bursting with wine" (Proverbs 3:9-10). We need to teach our kids to *honor the Lord* with their wealth and that the firstfruits (the tithe) always belong to Him.

38

We've already talked about the best way to do that – the 10/10/80 plan. Give 10 percent to God, put 10 percent in savings, and use 80 percent to live on. It's the best plan I know and the one I have followed most of my life.

I always encourage people to start there. If you want to give 12 percent or 18 percent to God, put 20 percent in savings, and live on the rest, that's your choice. As you grow and God blesses you, you can increase your giving and saving percentages and decrease your living expenses. But the place to start is the 10/10/80 plan. We all need to be doing it, and we need to be teaching our kids to do the same.

So how can we teach this plan to our kids, especially when they are very young? It's simple.

First, *honor the Lord*, and second, *follow God's plan*. We teach them that whatever God says to do, we do. We don't argue with God's plan. We don't try to modify God's plan. We don't find some other plan. We do what God says – we *follow His plan*.

FEED THE PIG

The third thing we teach our kids to do is *feed the pig*.

I'm sure you're wondering, *Feed the pig? What does that mean?* Feeding the pig is another way of saying children should be taught to put something into savings every week. (Adults should be doing this too!) To get on the road to financial freedom and stay there the rest of your life, you need to *feed the pig*. There are no ifs, ands, or buts about it. Whatever we can do to help kids or adults save something every week, we need to do it. A piggy bank is a great first step for kids. But the visual picture of feeding the pig every week is something that can benefit all of us.

Parents sometimes ask what their kids will use to *feed the pig*. That's where you come in. You knew there was a catch, right?

An extremely important part of our financial plan, of God's plan for us, is that we learn to save. Proverbs 13:11 says, "Wealth gained hastily will dwindle, but whoever gathers little by little will increase it."

It's better that we discipline ourselves and teach our kids to save something every week rather than play the lottery hoping they'll win. I know someone ultimately wins the lottery – and the fantasy that it could be *me* fuels the hopes and dreams of millions of people to foolishly finance the dreams of others.

Some people bank on the fact they'll get a huge inheritance from some relative they never knew, or they'll win the Publishers Clearing House Sweepstakes and get $5,000 a week for life.

Have you ever listened to the advertising? I might win $5,000 a week for life because I subscribe to *Good Housekeeping* or some other magazine. Again, someone wins. But the chances you or I will win are very small. (How many of your friends have retired on their winnings from the lottery or the $5,000 a week for life from Publishers Clearing House? That's what I thought.)

I saw a commercial once for IHOP that said, "Put on your stretchy pants and come see how many pancakes you can eat." When I heard that I thought, *They're not looking out for my best interests, but their own. They want to sell pancakes.*

The Bible says, "The rich rules over the poor, and the borrower is the slave of the lender" (Proverbs 22:7).

We need to teach our kids to be savers, not spenders – savers, not slaves to someone else, some financial institution, or borrowers from anyone. Teaching that to our kids is our responsibility as parents.

How do we do that? I recommend every parent teach their children how to manage money and how things work in the marketplace. Children should learn every bit of that at home. You may think you're way over your head and can't do that. If you're a mom or a dad, I don't care how old you are or how many kids you have, you can do this.

GIVE THEM JOBS (NOT CHORES)

Give your children jobs to do around the home. Don't call them *chores*. Call them *jobs*. Work is not a chore. It's a joy. It's a reward. Work is an opportunity to get on the road to financial freedom. Work is the highway that helps us get to where our dreams can come true.

Give them jobs, not chores.

A lot of people hate Mondays. And they don't know why. I think I know why. They must go to work, and they don't like work. If somebody would write them a check for a million dollars and they could quit work, and never work again, they would do it today.

Do you know why that's true for so many people? Because they had chores while growing up. Millions of people learned at an early age that working is not fun. It's a chore. Their parents made them do it, so it's a chore. Because they started out wrong with chores as a kid, many adults hate getting in the car and going to work on Mondays.

So, don't call them *chores*. Call them *jobs*. We want to teach our kids the right thing. We want to teach them that work is a blessing. Work can be fun. Work can help you accomplish your dreams.

If you have a job, thank God for it and do the best job you can, realizing that rewards come from working and doing a good job. That's what God teaches and that's what we want to teach our kids.

Give your children jobs and tell them you'll give them a paycheck every Friday. (For those of you who have just fallen on the floor, get back up and keep reading. It's going to be OK.)

By the way, don't call the paycheck an *allowance*. Many people were given an allowance when they were kids; maybe you were given one, too. That was another mistake because when you leave your home and go out into the world, no one makes allowances for you. There are no allowances.

But in the home, where we are always giving and making allowances,

41

we unintentionally develop an entitlement mentality in our kids that can cripple them and hinder them the rest of their lives. It's unintentional but permanent.

You don't want to live your life based on freebies, handouts, or government programs anyway. You want to earn your own way. You want to do your own job, and because you do your job and do it well, you get a paycheck.

It's also important to give your children a paycheck on Friday – not Tuesday, not Thursday – because in the marketplace, most people get paid on Friday. Remember, you're teaching your kids how to manage money and how the marketplace works. So, we need to do it that way.

When your kids are younger, write them a check. They need to see the check. Someone will say, "Nobody does that anymore. It's all done online." I get that, and when your kids are older they'll understand that and you can switch to making a direct deposit into their savings account. But starting out, you need to impress upon your kids: *You have a job, you do it well, and you get a paycheck. Every Friday.*

You're teaching your kids how to manage money and how the marketplace works.

Don't give them too many jobs or too much money or you'll provoke them to anger. Some parents will be tempted to outdo others and do more for their kids than any other parent. Just remember the warning of Proverbs 29:21: "If you pamper a servant in the beginning, he will bring you grief in the end" (paraphrased). Responsible kids emerge from responsible parents who take their responsibility responsibly.

Start simple and small. Let the paycheck match your child's age. If you have a 5-year-old, they have jobs and they work all week, and on Friday they get $5. If you have a 10-year-old, they have jobs, and if they work all week and do their job well, they get $10. Let the amount match their age. That's a great place to start for any family and for any child or teenager.

As an example, let's say you have a 5-year-old named Emma. We tell her: "Emma, you're going to have some jobs, and if you do your jobs every week, you're going to be paid $5 every Friday. You're going to get a paycheck. And Emma, when you keep doing your jobs well, as you get older, you'll get raises."

Remember, we're teaching them how the marketplace works. So we must teach them how to manage money – their finances – in a way that honors God and to help them understand how things work in the marketplace.

Next, open a savings account for your children. There are plenty of financial institutions, even Christian ones, to choose from. Open an account for them that will pay the highest rate of interest possible.

If you start young children with a piggy bank, when it gets full, take them to the bank or financial institution and show them how to deposit their money into their savings account.

By the way, if you're a grandparent, you can help with this, too. If your grandkids don't have savings accounts, go open accounts for them. No one will argue with you about that.

We teach our children they have to do their jobs and do them well to get their paycheck each week. If they don't do their jobs or don't do them right, they don't get paid. It's that simple.

So what jobs do we give little 5-year-old Emma? How would this work in real life? We start simple and start small. So we say, "Emma, we have three jobs for you, and if you do these three jobs every day of the week, you'll get a $5 paycheck every Friday.

"Here are your jobs, Emma. When you get up in the morning, we want you to make your bed. Every morning. Seven days a week. Not just three, not four. Seven days a week we want you to get up and make your bed. Number two, whenever you're done brushing your teeth, brushing your hair, and getting ready in the bathroom, we want you to wipe off the counter so it looks nice. And your third job is, whenever we have breakfast or lunch or dinner as a family, we want you to help clean the dishes off the table. That's it. Those are your three jobs. You do those three jobs, do them well every day of the week, and every Friday we're going to give you a paycheck. Five dollars."

As your kids get older, they can take on more jobs and their pay can increase. Of course, don't tell 5-year-old Emma she has to mow the lawn to earn her five bucks. Remember: God doesn't want us to provoke our kids to anger.

As your kids get older, you can give them age-appropriate jobs around the house. But every child, regardless of age, ought to have those three basic jobs: make their bed, wipe off the bathroom counter, and help clean the dishes off the table after meals.

What happens when they get paid on Friday? We're teaching them God's plan, so we start by telling them they need to *honor the Lord* – 10 percent to God. Tithe.

"Emma, here's your first paycheck. It's for $5. Fifty cents of that goes to God. We tithe. We give that to God through our church."

Don't tell Emma she can give that 10 percent to United Way or the Red Cross or the Girl Scouts or Kohl's. Corporations have learned when they tell people something such as, "If you buy this barbecue grill or this appliance or some other product, we'll give two percent of the price to help restore the rainforests," people are more prone to purchase the thing they are trying to sell because everyone wants to feel good about their purchase.

The firstfruits – the tithe – belong to God and it's to be given to *His* house – the tabernacle and temple in the Old and New Testaments and the local church today. God's church is the storehouse. (It's not your house, my house, or some other house.) We need to teach our kids that 10 percent of whatever

God gives us we give back to Him as a tithe.

The second thing we tell them – or Emma, in this case – is they need to put 10 percent into savings. Remember, we're following the 10/10/80 plan. Whether the child is *feeding the pig* or you're using direct deposit, 10 percent goes to God – we *honor the Lord* first – and the next 10 percent goes to savings.

You're free to do whatever you want with the remaining 80 percent. For instance, if little Emma wants to give more to God, don't discourage her. If she wants to put more in savings, don't stop her. We don't ever want to discourage anyone from doing those two things, but we also want to teach them correctly.

Teach them to save money for special purchases, because we're not going to give them everything anymore. No more allowances. That's not the way the world works. Parents actually save money in the long run by doing this. Yes, there will be an occasional gift, but no allowances.

If you are a parent, and you set up the 10/10/80 plan with jobs and paychecks, and the discipline to follow through on it every week, your kids won't like it initially. Right now, in most homes, kids have a sweet deal. They just ask or beg their parents for money – or throw a temper tantrum – and they have learned they can get whatever they want. But that's not the way the world works.

At times you give your children gifts they didn't earn, for their birthday or Christmas, for instance. Or someday you might come home from work and find you're so thankful they've done their jobs and they've become great young men and great young women who are *following God's plan*, that you decide to reward them. That's OK.

But we need to tell our kids, "If you want to go to that movie, you need to save money for it. If you want that jacket, you need to save money for it." And even though it's hard at first, they'll start learning how life works.

When your child turns 16, the paychecks stop. Now it's time for them to go out into the marketplace and get a real job. Where does the $15 a week you've been paying go now? It goes into *your* savings account. This is one of the best parts: You've already disciplined yourself every week, so now you've got $780 a year you can put in your own savings account. It's a phenomenal deal because you've disciplined yourself to gather little by little while you were teaching your kids to do the same.

Once your kids get their own jobs, you don't have to worry about them because you've taught them how to manage their money and how the marketplace works. You've taught them the 10/10/80 plan. And they're going to be excited about going to work early because you've taught them work is a joy, a blessing, and a way to accomplish their dreams. It's the way to get on the road to financial freedom.

They're going to come home from their new job and say, "Mom, Dad, look at this paycheck I got. I can't believe what they paid me!" And you'll ask them, "What are you going to do with all of that money?" What do you think your teenager will say after all those years of teaching, training, modeling, and encouraging? It will be something like this: "I'm going to do what you taught me. The first 10 percent goes to God. It's a tithe. The next 10 percent goes into savings and because I really don't have any bills right now, I'm going to put the rest of it into savings to someday buy a car."

You've taught your children how to manage their money and how things work in the marketplace. You've helped them get on the road to financial freedom. What parent wouldn't want that for their kids?

Let's look ahead a few years. Let's say Emma is 40 years old now and the CEO of a corporation. She's successful, wealthy, and owns her own business. She's holding a meeting with all her employees sitting in front of her. She says, "We've got a great team of employees and a great company. I appreciate all of you and everything you do. All of you work hard at your jobs, and I'm sure you want to instill that same trait in your children. That's why I want to tell you this story.

"When I was a little girl, my parents gave me three jobs to do every day, and they taught me to do my jobs well. My parents taught me that work is a joy, it's fun, it's a way to accomplish my dreams, and that's why I love coming to work here every day. I absolutely love it. My parents also taught me the 10/10/80 plan. I don't know if you've ever heard of that, but I'd like for all of you, as my employees, to at least try it.

"Here's how it works: The first 10 percent goes to God. It goes to the Lord's house, His storehouse – the local church. The next 10 percent goes to savings, and you live on the other 80 percent. If you have kids at home, I encourage you to teach them as my parents taught me. Teach them the 10/10/80 plan. Teach them to *honor the Lord, follow God's plan,* and *feed the pig.*"

Can you imagine the impact?

START A MOVEMENT

That's all you need to do, Mom and Dad, to change Emma's life – to change the lives and trajectory of your children's future. You're likely to start a chain reaction that will change the lives and futures of all kinds of people, all because you decided that instead of provoking your children to anger, you want to do what God said and bring your children up in the discipline and instruction of the Lord.

One more thing: When your kids turn 16, they will continue to do their jobs at home. Why? Because of the three Rs: roof over your head, refrigerator in the kitchen, and running water. They understand how to manage their money and how the marketplace works (because you taught them), and they also understand sometimes you do stuff because that's who you are and you're part of a family.

Imagine Emma at age 19. She's away at college, staying in a home of some friends. She gets up in the morning and makes the bed. No guest has ever stayed in that home and made the bed. But Emma does, and her friends are blown away. When she's done in the bathroom she wipes the counter and makes it look better than it did before she arrived. When the friends finish breakfast, Emma is the first one to get up and help with the dishes. Those friends have never met anyone like Emma. Where did she learn all that? At home.

Maybe as you read this, you're regretting that your kids are already grown and you didn't teach them these things. Please understand, it's never too late. Sit down with them and explain, "Even at your age, even though you're grown, this could change your life."

If you're a grandparent, do everything you can to encourage your kids to *follow God's plan* and to understand the importance of the 10/10/80 plan. Teach your grandchildren too!

If you are single, or perhaps a widow or widower, it's never too early or too late. Get your financial house in order. Get on the road to financial freedom so you can help others.

God's plan is for every one of us. So are His blessings. And if you want to receive His blessings and enjoy them, you've got to *honor the Lord, follow God's plan*, and *feed the pig*!

- We need to remember what a family is supposed to do.

- We need to honor the Lord and follow His plan.

- We need to feed the pig – put something in savings every week.

- Parents should give their kids jobs (not chores) and paychecks (not allowances).

- Parents should teach their kids how things work with money and in the marketplace.

- Parents should teach their kids how to honor the Lord and follow His plan.

- We should get on the road to financial freedom not only to help ourselves, but also to help others.

DID YOU KNOW...
 "The first power windows, which used a hydro-electric mechanism, were introduced in the 1940 Packard 180 series automobiles and were considered strictly as a luxury option."

(Source: https://www.kbb.com/what-is/power-windows/)

I've met a lot of people like
the rich fool in Luke 12.
They beg God for His blessing and
then, when the blessings come,
they tell God to "butt out!"

BLC

4

SIGNS, LINES, AND FINES

Bernie Madoff was back in the news again. According to Fox News in 2017, he was wheeling and dealing again, this time in prison – the Butner Federal Correctional Institution outside of Raleigh, North Carolina. Word came that Madoff somehow bought up all of the hot cocoa mix in the commissary. I don't know how the guy does it, but he bought it all. So, if you wanted hot chocolate, you had to go through Madoff.[7]

In March 2009, Madoff had pleaded guilty to operating the largest Ponzi scheme ever. Specifically, he pleaded guilty to 11 felony counts, which included securities fraud, investment adviser fraud, money laundering, mail fraud, wire fraud, making false statements, perjury, making a false filing with the SEC, and committing theft from an employee benefit plan. He was sentenced to 150 years in prison, the maximum allowed.

A federal judge ordered Madoff to forfeit $170 billion in real estate, investments, and other assets to repay victims an estimated $65 billion lost in his scheme. (The $170 billion is equal to all of the money that ran through accounts linked to the fraud; as of 2018, about $13 billion had been recovered.) These dollar amounts stagger the imagination. It's amazing to think he started Bernard L. Madoff Investment Securities, LLC, in 1960, in

51

part with $5,000 he earned from a summer lifeguarding job and a side gig installing sprinkler systems.

Madoff's firm became famous – and ultimately, infamous – for claiming annual returns of 10 percent or more year after year.

According to a *Time* magazine report, Madoff never turned a profit on the money he was given, nor did he invest any of it.[8] If he would've taken some of that $170 billion and just put it on deposit at the bank, he would've had something to show for it. But he didn't even do that.

Among the people who lost money because of Madoff were Kevin Bacon, Kyra Sedgwick, Steven Spielberg, Sandy Koufax, Nobel Peace Prize recipient and Holocaust survivor Elie Wiesel, and a number of millionaires who should have known better.

Bernie Madoff is the perfect example of someone who ignored the signs, lines, and fines. Truth is, he fooled a lot of people. He served on a lot of boards for nonprofit institutions, many of which entrusted his firm with their endowments. He donated approximately $6 million to lymphoma research when his son was diagnosed with the disease, was involved with the Gift of Life Bone Marrow Foundation, and made philanthropic gifts through the Madoff Family Foundation, a $19 million private foundation he and his wife managed.

It all came crashing down in 2008. On December 10, he told his sons he wanted to pay out more than $100 million in bonuses months ahead of schedule. When his sons challenged the idea, he said, "Let's go to my apartment." Once they got there, he confessed to the scam. "It's all been one big lie," he said.

The following morning, December 11, federal agents arrested Madoff.[9]

When you take money that doesn't belong to you and use it for yourself or give it to someone else, that's not genius or generosity. That's robbery. That's a crime. Bernie Madoff took money that did not belong to him and indulged himself, his family, and his friends. Then he attempted to keep the scheme going by using monies from new investors to fund payouts to earlier investors.

It worked for a while. He lived like a king for years, but he got caught, pleaded guilty, and was sentenced. On the day of sentencing, June 29, 2009, he apologized to his victims and said, "I have left a legacy of shame."

Madoff will forever be remembered as one of the biggest financial frauds in U.S. history. Part of his legacy will be the suicide of one of his sons on the second anniversary of Madoff's arrest.

What a mess.

BE WISE

Bernie Madoff's story clearly demonstrates that money can do peculiar things to people, including you and me. The Bible warns, "For the love of money is a root of all kinds of evils. [Money itself is not the problem; it's *the love of money*.] It is through this craving that some have wandered away from the faith and pierced themselves with many pangs" (1 Timothy 6:10).

Money can keep people out of church, away from God, and in all kinds of trouble. The Bible says, "Keep falsehood and lies far from me; give me neither poverty nor riches, but give me only my daily bread. Otherwise, I may have too much and disown you and say, 'Who is the Lord?' Or I may become poor and steal, and so dishonor the name of my God" (Proverbs 30:8-9, *NIV*). That's great advice. Money can do some peculiar things if you're not careful.

Money should never be the pursuit of our lives. God should be. Jesus said, "Seek first the kingdom of God and his righteousness, and all these things will be added to you" (Matthew 6:33). Solomon said, "Cast but a glance at riches, and they are gone, for they will surely sprout wings and fly off to the sky like an eagle" (Proverbs 23:5, *NIV*). He also said, "Whoever trusts in his riches will fall, but the righteous will flourish like a green leaf"

(Proverbs 11:28).

When it comes to money, we should always rely on God's wisdom. There's a great story in 1 Kings 3 where God said to Solomon, "You can ask me for anything." Imagine if God said the same thing to you. What would you ask for? Solomon asked God for wisdom.

He said, "God, I just want wisdom to lead your people." In that same chapter, God said to him, "Moreover, I will give you what you have not asked for – both wealth and honor – so that in your lifetime you will have no equal among kings. And if you walk in obedience to me and keep my decrees and commands as David your father did, I will give you a long life" (1 Kings 3:13-14, *NIV*).

Did you catch that? Who gives wealth and honor and a long life? Where does that come from? IBM? Apple? Google? No, no, and no. The only One who can give it is God. That's why every one of us needs His wisdom.

God has given us everything we need to know in His Word. But instead of giving us unlimited riches, He has given us an unbelievable road to travel. On this road that belongs to Him, He reveals His wisdom to us. James 1:5 says, "If any of you lacks wisdom, let him ask God, who gives generously to all without reproach."

We can gain God's blessing during our travels, but there are also some rules and restrictions on that road. Every road has signs, lines, and fines.

We might protest, "But, I don't like all the lines. I don't like driving inside of them. And I don't like all of the obnoxious signs. I wish they'd take them down." That's too bad. You had better follow the rules or you'll pay a price.

There's a reason that sign has a curved arrow on it. It means the road is turning, and if you don't pay attention, you'll end up in a ditch.

If you've driven up Pikes Peak in Colorado, as I have, you know there are guardrails along the roadside as you start your drive, but they disappear as you get higher. The first time I realized that, I thought, *What fool did this? I mean, the higher we get the more treacherous the road gets. Why no guardrails?*

An annual race goes up Pikes Peak. Cars go incredibly fast and somehow navigate the curves without falling off the side of the mountain. But for my money (and sanity), I'd prefer to have guardrails.

We made the trip up Pikes Peak one winter's day; that probably was unwise. My younger brother from Florida was driving a van, traversing snow and ice. I was okay as long as there were guardrails, but when they disappeared, I said, "We need to turn around." My brother kept driving, but thankfully, authorities had closed the upper portion of the road because of snow. They made us turn around. I sat and prayed, "Thank You, God! Thank You, thank You, thank You."

Guardrails are there for a reason. Don't get upset about guardrails.

The same thing is true on the road to financial freedom. There are guardrails, signs, lines, and fines. God owns the road and makes the rules, and those rules are found in His Word.

What if you don't want to do it God's way? Truth is, you can do it your way or somebody else's way, and you might get away with it for a while. But, as Bernie Madoff discovered, you won't get away with it forever.

God is not trying to limit us. He is trying to protect us. Limits don't limit us and restrictions don't restrict us. Limits and restrictions actually protect us and provide us the safest means of travel.

Why do we need a road to financial freedom? Roads help us get to where we need to go. Roads make life easier. They actually make everything else in life possible. Every road has lines and we need to stay between those lines. Every road has signs. We need to obey those signs. If we ignore the lines and the signs, we have to pay the fines.

Jesus talked about two other roads in the Bible. He talked about a road that leads to eternal life and a road that leads to eternal destruction. He said we better make sure we're on the right road.

Some people say, "All roads lead to Heaven." But Jesus was clear: There are two roads. One leads to eternal life. The other leads to eternal damnation.

By the way, the road less traveled is the road to eternal life. The road to financial freedom is the road less traveled, as well. The majority of people are not on the road to financial freedom. They're not managing the resources God has given them His way or according to His Word.

Even though the Bible is clear everything belongs to God, many people, including some Christians, are still trying to do it like Frank Sinatra, "My Way" instead of God's way.

Let me remind you again – we might get away with it for a while, but we won't get away with it forever.

On the road to financial freedom, we've already seen we need to *honor the Lord*. That's where it all begins. In fact, the overarching principle of everything we do is this: If we *honor the Lord*, everything else will go better.

We also have to *follow His plan*. We have to do what God says.

Then, we need to *feed the pig*. We have to be disciplined, consistent savers.

Next, we need to *be faithful*.

BE FAITHFUL

I know some of you might be thinking, *If God owns it all and has it all, and if we're His children, why doesn't He just make us all rich?* The reason He doesn't do that is because He wants to know if we can *be faithful*.

That's illustrated by the parable of the talents in Matthew 25, which is actually a parable about trust. Jesus said,

> For it will be like a man going on a journey, who called
> his servants and entrusted to them his property. To one he

gave five talents, to another two, to another one, to each according to his ability. Then he went away. He who had received the five talents went at once and traded with them, and he made five talents more. So also he who had the two talents made two talents more. But he who had received the one talent went and dug in the ground and hid his master's money. Now after a long time the master of those servants came and settled accounts with them. And he who had received the five talents came forward, bringing five talents more, saying, "Master, you delivered to me five talents; here, I have made five talents more." His master said to him, "Well done, good and faithful servant. You have been faithful over a little; I will set you over much. Enter into the joy of your master." And he also who had the two talents came forward, saying, "Master, you delivered to me two talents; here, I have made two talents more." His master said to him, "Well done, good and faithful servant. You have been faithful over a little; I will set you over much. Enter into the joy of your master." He also who had received the one talent came forward, saying, "Master, I knew you to be a hard man, reaping where you did not sow, and gathering where you scattered no seed, so I was afraid, and I went and hid your talent in the ground. Here, you have what is yours." But his master answered him, "You wicked and slothful servant! You knew that I reap where I have not sown and gather where I scattered no seed? Then you ought to have invested my money with the bankers, and at my coming I should have received what was my own with interest. So take the talent from him and give it to him who has the ten talents. For to everyone who has will more be given, and he will have an abundance. But from the one who has not, even what he has will be taken away. And cast the worthless servant into the outer darkness. In that place there will be weeping and gnashing of teeth" (Matthew 25:14-30).

The word *talent* represents a measure of weight.

So in this story, the master gave an incredible amount of money to the first servant, a significant amount to the second servant, and a small amount to the third servant.

I want to be very clear about this: *We are not treated equally by God.* You can jump and shout and dance about. You can protest and argue all you want about your rights and privileges and what you ought to have and how we all ought to be equal. But the fact is, God doesn't treat us that way.

When it comes to salvation, there is neither Jew nor Greek, slave nor free, neither male nor female (Galatians 3:28).

When it comes to life, however, God gives to people according to their ability. Jesus made that clear in this parable. In other words, you and I determine what we have. We are not given the same opportunities. We are given what God can trust us with. *Our level of trust determines our level of treasure.* The important point isn't how many opportunities we have been given, but what we *do* with what we've been given.

We are all God's servants (Matthew 25:14) and we have one job, and that's to do whatever the Master says to do.

I love the story in the Gospel of John about the wedding in Cana in Galilee where Jesus turned water into wine, the first miracle He ever performed. The best part of the story is not when Jesus turned the water into wine; it's when Mary, Jesus' mother, told the servants, "Whatever Jesus says to do, do it." When the Master tells us to do something, we obey.

Let's get back to the parable of the talents.

We've been entrusted with the Master's property (v. 14). It all belongs to Him. Jesus made it clear, everything these servants had was entrusted to them from their master. We've already seen from Psalm 24:1, *it all belongs to God.*

Our level of trust determines our level of treasure (v. 15). Like I said earlier, you can shout and scream all you want about equality and equal treatment, but as we see in this parable, each person's level of trust determines their level of treasure. The way to more treasure is to increase our level of trust . . . by being faithful.

He lets us do whatever we want with what He gives us (v. 18). The master didn't tell them, "I gave you this talent. Now here's what you must do with it." No, he let them decide. God doesn't make us a bunch of robots. He gives us choices. He says, "Here, I'll give you these opportunities, abilities, and resources, and I want to see what you can do with them."

Our response can be either faithfulness or unfaithfulness.

What are you doing with the abilities and opportunities God's given you? Are you complaining because somebody else got more abilities and more opportunities? Are you mad because somebody else is treated in a different manner than you? Or are you being faithful with what God has given you regardless of what anybody else is doing? These are days of great opportunity for all of us, and we ought to *be faithful* with whatever God has given us.

God wants a return on His investment in us (v. 27). The master commended the first two servants for doubling what he had given them, but he rebuked the third servant for digging a hole in the ground and burying it. The master said, "You should have at least put that money on deposit with the bankers."

That's what Bernie Madoff should have done. An estimated $170 billion came through his account. If given the opportunity, I would have advised him to put some of that money in the bank and at least earn some interest on it. In fact, with that huge amount of money he might have earned enough interest to have satisfied many, if not most, of the accounts that were outstanding when everything fell apart. He might not have gone to prison for so long.

The point of the story, according to Jesus, is this: If you're a Christian, at the very least, you ought to at least be doing the very least!

If you're a genuine Christian, you're never going to say, "I'll just do the very least I'm expected to do." That's not the way to live the Christian life. But Jesus rebuked this wicked servant for not even doing the very least he should have done.

How many people do you know who have buried their abilities and blown their opportunities? Even some people who profess to be Christians take what God gives them and blow it on themselves and somehow think that's what life is all about.

We'll be rewarded or punished based on what we did with what God gave us. The master praised and promoted the first two servants because they were faithful. Two times in two verses (vv. 21 and 23) he said, "You have been faithful over a little; I will set you over much. Enter into the joy of your master." They were praised and promoted for being faithful.

Do you want to be praised? Would you like to be promoted? *Be faithful.* And by the way, did you notice the two servants became leaders? Don't miss that. That's always the way it happens. Whether your name is Moses (and you're out tending sheep) or Joseph (and you're in a pit or a prison), just *be faithful* and watch what God does.

The rewards and punishment are unending. Jesus said, "For to everyone who has will more be given, and he will have an abundance" (vv. 29-30).

Let me explain abundance. If I asked you to take a piece of paper and write the dollar figure that would be "enough" to walk away from your job and be set for life, what would your number be? Think about that for a moment. If you wrote down a number, and then I left for a year and came back and again asked you to write down a number that would be "enough," that dollar figure would have gotten bigger.

How do I know that? Because no amount is ever going to be enough.

Years ago, when I became a youth minister, I transitioned from a position at McDonald's where I was making about $3 an hour. I got a job as a youth minister and the church started paying me $80 a week. I thought, *Man, I'm rich! Eighty bucks a week!*

I went back to college and would walk through the dorm and shout, "Anybody want to go get a steak dinner? It's on me." Guys would come out of their rooms and I'd take them to a steakhouse and buy their meal because I had all that money.

If you were to ask me today, "Is $80 a week enough?" I'd have to say no. Because no amount is ever enough.

Now consider this. Jesus says, "To everyone who has will more be given, and he will have an abundance" (v. 29). That means if you're going to have an abundance, you must be getting more and more and more and more. If you're faithful, God's going to bless you and He will keep blessing you. That's what abundance is about.

"But from the one who has not, even what he has will be taken away. And cast the worthless servant into the outer darkness. In that place there will be weeping and gnashing of teeth" (vv. 29-30). It gets worse and worse. Why? Because that servant didn't faithfully manage the resources God gave him.

Jesus made it clear that this third servant was not only *unfaithful*, he was *faithless*.

Judas Iscariot was a disciple of Jesus. Even an apostle. You can't get closer to Jesus than Judas was. Someone says, "Well, I'm a member of a church." Let's be clear, Judas was closer to Jesus than that. He was as close as someone could be, and still he went to Hell. He was unfaithful – he betrayed the Lord.

A lot of people are still betraying Jesus today, and still because of money. Money can do peculiar things to people. It did to Judas. It still does to people today. That's why Jesus said, "And then will I declare to them, 'I never knew you; depart from me, you workers of lawlessness'" (Matthew 7:23).

Many people say they're Christians and they're going to Heaven. Yet they've taken God's money and, like a band of thieves, they're spending it all on themselves and thinking it doesn't matter. They are like Bernie Madoff, who thought he could stay one step ahead of federal agents and investigators forever.

The ramifications of how we manage what God gives us are eternal. That's why we need to *be faithful*. Money and possessions are a test. Rick Warren said,

> Most people fail to realize that money is both a *test* and a *trust* from God. God uses finances to teach us to trust him, and for many people, money is the greatest test of all. God watches how we use money to test how trustworthy we are. The Bible says, "If you are untrustworthy about worldly wealth, who will trust you with the true riches of heaven?" . . .
>
> God says there is a direct relationship between how I use my money and the quality of my spiritual life. How I manage my money ("worldly wealth") determines how much God can trust me with spiritual blessings ("true riches"). . . .
>
> Life is a test and trust, and the more God gives you, the more responsible He expects you to be.[10]

God is testing us to see if we can be trusted. Jesus said, "Whoever can be trusted with very little can also be trusted with much, and whoever is dishonest with very little will also be dishonest with much. . . . And if you have not been trustworthy with someone else's property, who will give you property of your own?" Then He adds, "No one can serve two masters. Either you will hate the one and love the other, or you will be devoted to the one and despise the other. You cannot serve both God and money" (Luke 16:10-13, *NIV*).

God gives us only what we can be trusted with, and He expects us to do something with it.

Christians ought to be the most faithful people on the planet. We ought to be as reliable as the sunrise, as faithful as our Father, who has entrusted us with every good thing.

Look again at 1 Timothy 6:7: "For we brought nothing into the world, and we cannot take anything out of the world." Do you know what God does between those two events – your entry date and your exit date – both set by Him? The answer comes 10 verses later: "[God] richly provides us with everything to enjoy" (1 Timothy 6:17). Don't miss this. We brought nothing in and we'll take nothing out. So in between being born and dying, God gives us everything to enjoy. God steps back and says, "I'm watching to see what you can do. That's it. *Be faithful.*"

So here's the bottom line: Obey the signs, stay within the lines, and avoid the fines. In other words: *Honor the Lord, follow God's plan, feed the pig, and be faithful.*

- Money makes people do funny things.

- When it comes to our finances, God has given us guardrails to protect us and signs to direct us.

- Roads help us get where we need to go and the road to financial freedom will help us get where we want to go.

- We need to be faithful.

- God wants a return on whatever He gives us.

- There are rewards or punishments based on what we do with what God gives us.

- Money and possessions are a test. God is testing us to see if we can be trusted.

DID YOU KNOW...
"In the early days of the automobile, air conditioning wasn't an option. In 1939, Packard produced the first cars with factory A/C: the 1940 Senior 160 and 180."

(Source: https://thenewswheel.com/when-did-cars-first-get-air-conditioning/)

Too many people give God what's left,
not what's right, and that's wrong.

BLC

5

GIVE ME THE KEYS

No right-minded parent would give the car keys to a teenage son or daughter who was insubordinate and fought against their authority. Just because someone's old enough to drive doesn't mean they're wise enough. Someone rebelling against authority in a home will have trouble submitting to authority on a highway or any road for that matter.

Fighting can be deadly.

Two moose were found frozen in about eight inches of ice near a remote village. They were found by Brad Webster, a science and social studies teacher from Unalakleet, Alaska. According to the Associated Press, he had taken a walk with a friend who had recently moved to the village. They were going to a frozen slough at Covenant Bible Camp, where Webster volunteered as a camp steward. The two moose were lying on their sides, antlers locked, apparently from a fight to the death.

Upon closer examination, it appeared one moose may have punctured the other's skull, and when he died, because their antlers were locked, the weight of the dead moose pulled the living moose into the cold water, where he froze to death.

"Male moose compete for females by clashing antlers and pushing against each other during the fall breeding season," said Kris Hundertmark, chair of the Biology and Wildlife Department at the University of Alaska Fairbanks. "Adult male moose are extremely strong, but their large antlers often have complex shapes that can become so entangled that the animals cannot dislodge themselves from their opponents."

He said he'd seen skulls of conjoined moose found in the wild, but not in ice.[11]

Two moose. Dead in the frozen water. Because they were fighting.

Bill Samuel, a retired biologist and moose expert at the University of Alberta in Canada, said he had never seen anything quite like it.[12]

But I have. Not with moose, but with people who fight God when it comes to their finances. They end up dead in the water because, instead of following what God says to do, they'd rather fight.

We've been learning how to *follow God's plan* instead of fighting it. So far, we've seen it all begins when we *honor the Lord*. Next, we need to *follow God's plan*. Then, we need to *feed the pig*.

When I began writing this book, my two grandsons, Will and Levi, were 8 and 5. One night the two of them were at our house for dinner. They love getting to hang out with Grandpa and Mayme, and we love it, too. We were eating dinner, and all of a sudden I noticed Levi, only three at the time, get down, grab his plate off the table, walk over behind Mayme, open up the trash can, and scrape the food scraps off his plate with a fork. He threw his napkin in, put his cleaned plate on the counter, and quietly headed out and started playing.

Will did the same thing. These two young guys are doing their jobs, even when they are with their grandparents. Why? Because their parents are teaching them. They're following the 10/10/80 plan, giving the tithe back to God every week, and learning how to manage their money and how things work in the marketplace.

Every child needs to learn that, and every parent needs to be teaching that. You and I don't need to try to improve on God's plan. We just need to get in on it. He knows what He's talking about. He's the creator of everything and has given us the Bible – a manual for managing our money and everything else in our lives.

It's not that hard if we listen to Him and *follow His plan*. However, there are some who'd rather be like a moose and fight it, which makes no sense at all. You're only hurting yourself.

The fourth thing we need to do is *be faithful*.

How we manage the resources God gives us has eternal ramifications – either eternal rewards or eternal punishment. Jesus said the servant who was unfaithful was cast out into the outer darkness where there was weeping and gnashing of teeth.

Someone asked me, "Now, I want to make sure here, you're not saying if someone doesn't manage their resources right, that they could end up going to Hell, are you?"

"No, that's not what I said."

"Good, I'm glad you didn't say that."

"No, I didn't say that. Jesus did."

This is serious stuff. It's eternally stupid to fight God's plan. The smart thing is to *follow God's plan* and *be faithful* all the days of our lives. How do we do that? We *bring the tithe*. Jesus said, "Therefore render to Caesar the things that are Caesar's, and to God the things that are God's" (Matthew 22:21). How did people in Caesar's day know what things belonged to Caesar? Caesar told them. How did people know what things were God's? God told them. He always has.

The tithe is 10 percent of whatever we receive. It's the firstfruits and it belongs to God.

Author and pastor Mark Batterson wrote,

> [Romans 8:23] says we have the "firstfruits" of the Spirit. Interesting word choice. Its etymology is agricultural, referencing Israel's two harvests. After the first harvest, the Israelites would take a firstfruits offering to the temple. According to Levitical law, if they honored God with the firstfruits, then God would bless the second harvest.
>
> The principle of firstfruits is a high leverage point.
>
> God doesn't want your leftovers. He wants the firstfruits. The tithe isn't any 10 percent. It's the *first* 10 percent. And when we honor God by giving the firstfruits back to Him, it invokes a blessing on the latter harvest. It's our 100 percent, money-back guarantee, complete with a lifetime warranty.

"Twenty-two years ago," Batterson wrote, "Lora and I made a defining decision that we would never *not* tithe. We've had our lean years, but God has proven faithful time and again. The old saying is true: you can't out-give God. But it sure is fun trying. I'm absolutely convinced that God can do more with 90 percent than I can do with 100 percent, and you can take that to the bank."[13]

Let me answer some common questions about tithing, because I don't want anyone reading this book to be fighting God and end up dead in the water . . . or frozen in the ice.

WHY DOES THE DEVIL FIGHT US SO HARD WHEN IT COMES TO TITHING?

Have you ever wondered why tithing is such a battle? The simple answer is that the devil doesn't want you and me connected to the unlimited resources of God. He doesn't want us to know how great God is – how God can meet every need of our lives. The devil wants us to believe God is not enough. But the simple truth is this: When you begin to tithe, you'll quickly discover, not only is God enough, He's more than enough.

WHEN DID THE TITHING BATTLE BEGIN?

Did you know the first murder in all of human history was over tithing and firstfruits?

Talk about people fighting God's plan. The first murder is found in Genesis 4. The Bible says, "Cain brought to the Lord an offering of the fruit of the ground, and Abel also brought of the firstborn of his flock and of their fat portions. And the Lord had regard for Abel and his offering, but for Cain and his offering He had no regard. So Cain was very angry, and his face fell" (Genesis 4:3-5).

They both brought an offering, but Abel brought the firstborn while Cain grabbed some leftover fruit and brought that to God. They both were giving something – wasn't that good enough? No. Why not? Because that's not what God said to do.

It's ironic Cain got mad about that. It's like the old saying, "Some people create their own storms and then complain about the rain." That was Cain.

In the next few verses, God rebuked Cain for doing his own thing and not doing what he was supposed to do. He didn't bring the firstfruits. So Cain killed his brother, Abel. Rather than admit his own mistake, rather than confess and say, "I'm wrong, I need to start doing what's right," Cain just got rid of Abel.

Want to know how that works today? Instead of killing someone, people won't read the Bible, or they will go to another church where they don't have to give anything. Instead of hearing about tithing, instead of *following God's plan*, they'll find a place where some false teacher makes them feel good about not doing what God says to do.

The problem is, someday every one of us is going to step out into eternity and answer to God for why we didn't do what He said to do. That's the point Jesus was making in the parable of the talents. How we manage what God gives us is serious business. Eternity is involved.

God said, "You shall have no other gods before me" (Exodus 20:3). That's the first of the Ten Commandments. Yet here, in this incredible country in which we've been blessed to live, the United States of America, we have an unlimited number of gods we can choose from. But there's One (and only One) we better choose because our eternity hangs in the balance on that choice.

HOW DID PEOPLE KNOW WHAT THEY WERE SUPPOSED TO GIVE?

God told the people what to give. He always has and always will. Long before the Law, long before the Old Testament, and long before the New Testament was written, God taught Cain and Abel about the firstfruits. Somehow God had told them, "This is what belongs to me. You're to bring the firstfruits, the best. I don't want everything. I just want the best of what I bless you with. I want you to acknowledge that I am God, that I am Lord."

The firstfruits have always belonged to God and they always will. It's not legalism. It's not law. It's lordship.

How did people in New Testament times know what belonged to Caesar? When Jesus said, "Give to Caesar what belongs to Caesar," how did they know what that was? It's because Caesar made it clear to them. We don't have Caesar today. Instead, we have Uncle Sam, which sounds like the name of a lovable family member, but really is a play on the initials U.S. (meaning the United States government).

Something else that's interesting to note: From the beginning, whether we're talking about Caesar, Uncle Sam, or God, the "giving" always involves a percentage. But while Caesar and Uncle Sam had (or have) tax rates that keep changing, the percentage God asks of us has never changed. From the very beginning, God has always asked for the first 10 percent. That is to be the bottom line, not the finish line, for our giving.

WHAT DID JESUS SAY ABOUT TITHING AND GIVING THE FIRSTFRUITS?

The answer to this question is found in the Sermon on the Mount, the greatest sermon ever preached. I've actually stood where Jesus preached that sermon, the very place He made two amazing declarations. The first is found in Matthew 5:17: "Do not think that I have come to abolish the Law or the Prophets; I have not come to abolish them but to fulfill them." Oftentimes people say, "Well, that's Old Testament" or "We're not under that anymore." Listen, Jesus didn't come to abolish them. He came to fulfill them.

The second amazing declaration comes two verses later: "Therefore whoever relaxes one of the least of these commandments and teaches others to do the same will be called least in the kingdom of heaven, but whoever does them and teaches them will be called great in the kingdom of heaven" (5:19). In other words, "I didn't come to lower expectations, I came to raise them."

And then Jesus gave examples of raising expectations (and not lowering them).

"You have heard that it was said to those of old, 'You shall not murder; and whoever murders will be liable to judgment.' But I say to you that everyone who is angry with his brother will be liable to judgment" (Matthew 5:21-22).

Jesus didn't come to lower that expectation. He raised it.

"You have heard that it was said, 'You shall not commit adultery.' But I say to you that everyone who looks at a woman with lustful intent has already committed adultery with her in his heart" (vv. 27-28).

He didn't lower that expectation. He raised it.

"You have heard that it was said, 'An eye for an eye and a tooth for a tooth.' But I say to you . . ." (vv. 38-39). And Jesus goes on to encourage us not to seek revenge or retaliation, but to go the second mile with people.

He didn't lower the expectation. He raised it.

What does it mean to go the second mile? Under Roman law, if a soldier came to your house or dwelling, you were required to carry his backpack for a mile. So a Jewish boy would measure out a mile from his house in every direction and put a stake down so he knew exactly how far it was. When a soldier showed up, the boy would carry that soldier's backpack until he reached the stake, and he'd just drop it there. He was under no obligation to carry it another step. That's all the law required him to do.

But Jesus said, "No. That may be lawful, but let me tell you about lordship. I want you to go the second mile. I want you to keep carrying that backpack so that the soldier says, 'Hey, what are you doing? Aren't you going to throw my backpack down?'

'No, I'll carry it some more for you.'

'You really don't have to do that.'

'It's okay, I'll carry it for you.'

"In time, the soldier will ask, 'Why are you doing this?' And you can reply, 'Because I'm a follower of Jesus.'"

Jesus didn't lower the expectations. He raised them.

Jesus went on to say, "You have heard that it was said, 'You shall love your neighbor and hate your enemy.' But I say to you, Love your enemies and pray for those who persecute you" (Matthew 5:43-44).

He didn't lower expectations. He raised them.

So, if Jesus didn't come to abolish the law and the prophets, and He came to raise expectations, not lower them, what does that say about *tithing*?

We have an answer from the lips of Jesus himself. Later in this same Gospel, Jesus said to the religious leaders, "Woe to you, scribes and Pharisees, hypocrites! For you tithe mint and dill and cumin [the three smallest spices known to man], and have neglected the weightier matters of the law: justice and mercy and faithfulness. These you ought to have done [tithing those spices], without neglecting the others" (Matthew 23:23).

Jesus reinforced the tithe while stressing matters of more importance, but which also fall under the tithe. Jesus said the religious leaders apparently were ignoring matters of first importance such as justice, mercy, and faithfulness. The Old Testament says "a tithe of everything belongs to the Lord" (Leviticus 27:30, *NIV*), and not just as it relates to spices.

If we don't tithe – if we don't follow God and we're not faithful to Him – then we're fighting Him. We're a moose and, if we keep fighting, we're going to end up a dead moose.

In his book *How to Have More than Enough,* Dave Ramsey says, "If you're not tithing, giving God the first 10 percent of your income – start today. Make your giving the first check you write, at the top of your budget. Have you ever considered that perhaps your failure to honor God off the top of your income is one of the reasons you've been struggling financially?"

Ramsey then says, "You may be thinking, 'Tithe? How am I supposed to give away ten percent of my income? I can barely pay my phone bill.' Then get rid of your phone, but don't rob God."[14]

The website of Prestonwood Baptist Church in Plano, Texas, led by my friend Jack Graham, says the purpose of tithing "is to teach us to put God first in our lives. God doesn't need our money. Instead, He wants what our money represents: our priorities, passions, purposes. Make a commitment to tithe and dedicate yourself to it. And more than anything . . . trust God and let Him prove His promises."[15]

WHERE DOES THE TITHE BELONG?

Tithing is giving back to God 10 percent of whatever He blesses us with financially. So where does the tithe belong? God's Word says, "Bring the whole tithe into the storehouse, that there may be food in my house. 'Test me in this,' says the Lord Almighty, 'and see if I will not throw open the floodgates of heaven and pour out so much blessing that there will not be room enough to store it'" (Malachi 3:10, *NIV*).

So what is the storehouse? Charles Stanley said the storehouse "meant His tabernacle or temple in the Old Testament, and the church in the New Testament. We are to give our tithes wherever we regularly worship the Lord – not only to care for the church building and those who work there, but to support the expansion of His kingdom by spreading the gospel and ministering to the community for His name's sake."[16]

No one eats at McDonald's and pays at Burger King. And I don't recommend trying it.

Here's my point: Many Christian people go to a church and, instead of tithing – giving the firstfruits back to God through their church – they say, "I support United Way" or "I give money to help save the rainforest" or "I sponsor needy children in Africa." But here's the reality: God says the tithe is to be brought to His storehouse, which is the local church.

The tithe belongs to God. It's the firstfruits. We don't get to *divert* it, *divide* it or *direct* it. It belongs to God.

I'm a pastor of a local church. So how would you feel if, when I gave my tithe to my church, I told the bookkeeper, "Now be sure and put this in the pastor's retirement account." Would you have a problem with that? I think virtually everyone would say that's not right.

Years ago, when I was a freshman in Bible college, I was sitting on the third row of Blendville Christian Church in Joplin, Missouri. It came time for the offering, and I had a tithe of what I'd made at McDonald's that week;

the tithe was in an envelope and I put it in the offering. My three friends who were sitting with me gave nothing. I asked, "Aren't you going to give something?" They said, "We already give to God's kingdom. When we pay on our school bill, that's going to the kingdom because it's a Bible college." I told them, "No, that's not how it works." Ironically, or maybe not, none of those guys are in ministry today.

No matter what anyone else says or how good it might sound, don't follow someone else's plan, because you'll wind up no better off than a dead moose frozen in the ice. And don't fight God's plan; don't get sidetracked from His road to financial freedom.

We have the privilege of bringing the tithe back to God every week. It's not a pain, it's a privilege to bring it to God's house, our local church.

My wife and I are online church givers and have been for years. If you haven't done it yet, I'd recommend you automate your giving (as well as your savings). Yet, every Sunday, I still put an envelope with extra above our tithe in one of the offering boxes at our church building. Maybe it's the traditionalist in me, but even more so, I like giving to be part of my Sunday worship.

SHOULDN'T WE GIVE WHAT WE DECIDE IN OUR HEARTS TO GIVE?

Some may ask, don't Paul's words, "Each of you should give what you have decided in your heart to give" (2 Corinthians 9:7, *NIV*), override the principle of tithing?

That's a great verse, but it has nothing to do with tithing and it certainly doesn't override or supersede it. The context of that verse was a love offering for the poor saints of Jerusalem. Paul was saying that each person could decide what they should give in that love offering.

When it comes to the tithe, God has already decided that. God said the firstfruits are always to be brought to Him, and it's 10 percent of whatever He has blessed us with – and the way we bring it to Him is through our local church.

A couple of final thoughts: In the same Sermon on the Mount, Jesus made several other powerful points about money and giving.

Jesus said, "Do not lay up for yourselves treasures on earth. . . . But lay up for yourselves treasures in heaven" (Matthew 6:19-20). Why would people want to try to keep everything for themselves? We've already talked about 1 Timothy 6:7, where Paul says we brought nothing into this world and we'll take nothing out of this world. But if you watch certain people, including church people, you'd think they'd figured out how to take it with them.

But they haven't, and they won't.

Billy Sunday, a professional baseball player who became a bold evangelist, has been quoted as saying, "If we could take it with us, it would melt where some of us are going."

Jesus said, "But lay up for yourselves treasures in heaven, where neither moth nor rust destroys and where thieves do not break in and steal" (Matthew 6:20). It's one of the rare times in Scripture where Jesus said to do something for yourself. Lay up for yourselves treasures in Heaven.

In Matthew 6:21, Jesus said, "For where your treasure is, there your heart will be also." Someone said you can give without loving, but you cannot love without giving. Jesus made it clear *what* we give and *how* we give reveals our hearts. Judging by the statistics of all the churches in America, and the statistics of the way people give, a lot of people are on spiritual life support. They're barely making it, and it shouldn't be that way.

Jesus said, "Don't worry about how you're going to get your needs met. My Father will meet them all" (Matthew 6:25, paraphrased). That's a great encouragement. We don't have to worry about our needs being met. Jesus said, "My Father will take care of you."

Paul said the same thing: "And my God will supply every need of yours according to his riches in glory in Christ Jesus" (Philippians 4:19).

Jesus said in summary, "Seek first the kingdom of God and his righteousness" (Matthew 6:33). It's all about lordship. It's not about law. It's not about legalism. It's not about money. It's about the Master. It's not about finances. It's about our faithfulness and whom we are following.

To put it another way: "Honor the Lord with your wealth and with the firstfruits of all your produce; then your barns will be filled with plenty, and your vats will be bursting with wine" (Proverbs 3:9-10).

If you're not ready to *tithe*, you're not ready to drive *on the road to financial freedom*.

So the bottom line to getting on the road to financial freedom and staying there the rest of our lives is this: *Honor the Lord, follow God's plan, feed the pig, be faithful,* and *bring the tithe.*

- We need to follow God's plan, not fight it.

- The Bible is a manual for managing our money and everything else in our lives.

- Young children should learn God's plan at the earliest age possible.

- There's a reason why the devil fights us so hard when it comes to tithing.

- The Bible is clear regarding how and what we are to give.

- Jesus didn't lower the standards, He raised them.

- The tithe belongs to God and is to be brought to the storehouse.

- The firstfruits belong to God. Anything above that we are free to give wherever we choose.

DID YOU KNOW...
"In 1973, Oldsmobile installed the first passenger airbag in a car called a 'Tornado.' Over twenty years later, in 1998, the federal government required all passenger vehicles to be equipped with standard, dual front airbags."

(Source: https://www.idrivesafely.com/defensive-driving/trending/evolution-automobile)

Getting out of debt was one of the greatest challenges we've ever faced as a family. But it was one of the best things we've ever done, and it was worth every sacrifice!

BLC

6

DETOUR AHEAD

It was a routine admission to busy Bellevue Hospital. A charity case. One among many from that section of New York City. A man from the Bowery had a sliced throat and a concussion.

The Bowery – last stop before the morgue. A place of filth, loneliness, poverty, cheap booze, and disease. The man's name was misspelled on the hospital registry. His age was also incorrect. He was 37, not 38. What a shame for someone so young to die in such a way, in such a place.

Chuck Swindoll tells the story, but the details of what happened that predawn winter morning in 1864 were fuzzy. The nurse would have seen hundreds of cases like this and would probably see hundreds more. Would it have mattered had she known who this man was? Probably so. His recent past was the polar opposite of his earlier years. The Bowery had become a dead-end stop for an incredible life. And, like most, he lived for his next drink more than his next meal. His health was gone, and he was starving.

On that icy morning, before the sun crept over the New York skyline, this shell of a man who looked twice his age and was suffering from a fever and ill health fell against a washbasin. The basin toppled and shattered. He was found bleeding from a gash in his neck and was only semiconscious.

The doctor used a simple sewing thread to suture the wound. That would have to do.

All the time he was being stitched up, he kept asking for a drink. He was placed in a paddy wagon and dumped off at Bellevue Hospital, where he would languish, unable to eat for three days, and then die alone. His friend, a drinking buddy, went looking for him, and was directed to the morgue. There, among dozens of colorless, nameless corpses with tags on their toes, he was identified.

Among his few belongings was a ragged, dirty coat with 38 cents in one pocket and a little scrap of paper in the other. That's all he possessed. Enough coins, perhaps, for another night in the Bowery and a little scrap of paper with five words, "Dear friends and gentle hearts." Like the words of a song.

Why in the world would this drunk carry a line of lyrics? Maybe he thought he still had it in him. Maybe this man, with the body of a bum, still had the heart of a musical genius. A few years before his tragic death, he had written songs known all over the world. Songs like "Camptown Races," "Oh! Susanna," "Jeanie With the Light Brown Hair," "Beautiful Dreamer," "Old Folks at Home," "My Old Kentucky Home," and 200 others that are deeply rooted in our rich American heritage.

The man nobody knew – who died alone – was Stephen Foster. What a tragic story. A man with such incredible gifts and abilities, all that God-given talent, yet he became a sad statistic because apparently he had lost all meaning and purpose in his life. At one time Stephen Foster was on the road to fame, fortune, financial freedom, and a fabulous future, but he took a fatal exit – a deadly detour that destroyed his life.[17]

How could someone who had so much, fall so far? Yet, it seems, stories of this sort have become almost cliché. Howard Hughes, Marilyn Monroe, Freddie Prinze, Elvis Presley, Natalie Wood, John Belushi, Len Bias, Kurt Cobain, Chris Farley, Anna Nicole Smith, Michael Jackson, Whitney

Houston – all died as victims of suicide or as victims of alcohol or drug abuse. Fatal exits. Deadly detours.

Others live today as victims of their own tragically poor choices – because they took the wrong exit, a detour: O.J. Simpson, Mike Tyson, Courtney Love, Eliot Spitzer, Bernie Madoff, Marion Jones, Barry Bonds, Tonya Harding, Bill Clinton, Lindsay Lohan, Anthony Weiner, Charlie Sheen, and the list goes on and on.

Sadder still is the fact millions of people today experience the same kind of defeat and futility, but you don't hear about them. Their lives may not end in suicide. Their names may never appear in headlines. But they're trying to escape the same dissatisfaction in life. They never know the victory, joy, and fulfillment God wants people to have.

No one has to live like that. There's a better way, a better road to travel: the road to financial freedom. And here's the good news: Every single person can get on that road. Including you.

How do we do it? *Honor the Lord, follow God's plan, feed the pig, be faithful, bring the tithe,* and *avoid the detours.*

Solomon said, "The rich rules over the poor, and the borrower is the slave of the lender" (Proverbs 22:7). Then he added, "Be not one of those who give pledges, who put up security for debts. If you have nothing with which to pay, why should your bed be taken from under you?" (vv. 26-27)

Earlier in that same book, Solomon said, "My son, if you have put up security for your neighbor, have given your pledge for a stranger, if you are snared in the words of your mouth, caught in the words of your mouth, then do this, my son, and save yourself, for you have come into the hand of your neighbor: go, hasten, and plead urgently with your neighbor. Give your eyes no sleep and your eyelids no slumber; save yourself like a gazelle from the hand of the hunter, like a bird from the hand of the fowler" (Proverbs 6:1-5).

Solomon was talking about debt. He was saying, "Don't even go to sleep. Get out of this."

Then he said, "Go to the ant, O sluggard; consider her ways, and be wise. Without having any chief, officer, or ruler, she prepares her bread in summer and gathers her food in harvest. How long will you lie there, O sluggard? When will you arise from your sleep? A little sleep, a little slumber, a little folding of the hands to rest, and poverty will come upon you like a robber, and want like an armed man" (Proverbs 6:6-11).

Dave Ramsey said, "Debt is so ingrained into our culture that most Americans can't envision a car without a payment, a house without a mortgage, a student without a loan, and credit without a card. We've been sold debt with such repetition and with such fervor that most folks can't conceive of what it would be like to have no payments."[18]

It hasn't always been that way. When I was growing up, no one I knew was in debt. I do recall, though, our country was in debt for billions of dollars. Fast forward to today. Now virtually everyone I know is in debt of some kind, and our country is more than $22 trillion in debt. Do I really need to tell you we're on the wrong road as a country and, for the most part, as individuals? We've taken a wrong turn. In some cases, several wrong turns. We've taken a detour away from God's plan.

Not that long ago in America, if you didn't have the cash to pay for something, you didn't buy it. Your parents and grandparents would tell you that you didn't need it or needed to save up the money before buying it. Now, for some reason, we've bought into the lie that if we want something, anything, we should just go get it. Even if we have to charge it or go into debt so we can have it. And here's the worst part: We call that *living*. But that couldn't be further from the truth.

Get this into your head and your heart: *Debt, rather than delivering your dreams, actually delays them and sometimes destroys them.*

Years ago I was a youth minister in Kansas City. A family in our church owned a phenomenal home that looked like a castle. They had phenomenal cars and phenomenal clothes. Everything they had was amazing. They were the envy of virtually everybody.

As a 22-year-old, I thought it was awesome, until one day their son told me it was all a lie. I asked him, "What do you mean, 'It's all a lie'?" He said, "We lease our home, lease our cars, we even lease our clothes – pretending to be people we aren't."

I was stunned.

A teenage boy told me this about his own family. But here's something equally amazing. I found out, over the years, a lot of people live in homes like that and drive cars like that. I don't know about the leasing clothes part. But a lot of people are living lies, trying to put on the dog and let everybody else know their doghouse is better than yours.

Why would anyone want to live like that? Why would anyone want to live a lie?

What is God's plan for His people when it comes to debt?

DEBT WAS NEVER GOD'S PLAN FOR HIS PEOPLE

I know it's a tough pill to swallow, but it's not God's plan for His people to be in debt, so do whatever is necessary to get it down. God revealed His plan in Deuteronomy 28:12: "You shall lend to many nations, but you shall not borrow." The *NIV* says, "You . . . will borrow from none." Yet today the United States has become like a third-world country in this respect. We are a debtor nation that owes money to a number of other countries.

How did it happen? God never intended for us to live in bondage to a business, builder, bank, or anyone else who would get rich off our debt.

When it comes to debt, virtually everyone has been there. We find ourselves sitting across the desk from the salesperson at the car dealership signing the papers and we're all excited, thinking we just got a great deal. Or we're sitting across the desk at a title company signing the papers on a big, new house and we're thinking, *This is awesome!* But we don't realize the truth: It's actually the people on the other side of the desk who've made the great deal because we're going to make them a lot of money.

Somehow we've been deceived into thinking debt is our friend. But the only good debt is a debt that's been paid off. We can afford to feel good about debt only when we reach the place where we're about to get out of it.

Debt is our way of giving ourselves what God hasn't given us yet. Instead of being patient, instead of *following His plan*, we come up with our own plan that ends up costing us more in the long run.

But if we could change the narrative in our lives and the lives of others, we could change everything. Especially if we change the narrative for our kids and grandkids. If we could get our kids and grandkids to do jobs (not chores) every week, give them paychecks (which they've earned) every Friday so they start learning how to manage their money and how things work in the marketplace, and teach them to follow the 10/10/80 plan, we will change the narrative.

Imagine this. If you paid cash for your first car, you'd be able to pay cash for every car you ever own. If you pay cash for your first house, you'll be able to pay cash for every house you ever own. You'll have a life without debt.

As a grandparent, I couldn't be more excited about what's happening for my two grandsons. They are on the road to financial freedom and on target to have lives that never depend on a single dime of debt.

Every parent should be excited for their children – that they don't follow the poorly chosen paths we have walked, but instead follow the path and plan given by Almighty God.

Debt was never God's plan for His people. Yet, rather than *following*

His plan, rather than *feeding the pig*, rather than *bringing the tithe*, we get impatient. We start thinking like Abraham and Sarah – that we need to help God out.

God told Abraham he would have a son who would be the father of many nations. But several years went by and nothing happened. So Abraham and Sarah said, "We need to help God out." And Sarah suggested, "Why don't you have a child with my handmaiden, Hagar?"

Abraham agreed to Sarah's suggestion. But when Hagar became pregnant, Sarah got upset and wanted Abraham to get rid of Hagar. The Bible says Sarah treated Hagar so badly that Hagar fled for her life out into the wilderness. "And the angel of the Lord said to her [Hagar], 'Behold, you are pregnant and shall bear a son. You shall call his name Ishmael, because the Lord has listened to your affliction. He shall be a wild donkey of a man, his hand against everyone and everyone's hand against him, and he shall dwell over against all his kinsmen'" (Genesis 16:11-12).

Do you know who Ishmael was? He was the father of all the Arab nations. Later on, Sarah gave birth to Isaac, the son God had promised. Through Isaac came the line of the Jewish nation.

So all of the problems in the Middle East today came about because two people thought they needed to help God out.

If you've been thinking you need to help God out, you should quickly and carefully reconsider. God doesn't need our help.

Debt was never God's plan for His people. Rather than delivering our dreams, debt actually delays them and, in some cases, destroys them.

THE BIBLE DOESN'T FORBID DEBT, BUT IT DOES DISCOURAGE IT

The fact is, when we go into debt, we become a slave to the one who lends to us. Proverbs 22:7 says, "The rich rules over the poor, and the borrower is the slave of the lender." And that means we have another master besides God.

Remember, Jesus said no man can serve two masters (Matthew 6:24; Luke 16:13), but most people don't think that verse applies to them. They've got their own thing going and they'll be fine. They know they're ignoring what God said to do, but they think He's going to bless them anyway.

When we go into debt, we obligate ourselves to someone other than God. And in many cases, our obligation to those financial institutions becomes greater, more pressing, more urgent, and more important than any obligation we have to God. So we end up moving God to the back of the line while still calling Him Lord.

Israelites made loans to their fellow Israelites, as Deuteronomy 15:2 makes clear. So it isn't wrong to have a loan. Deuteronomy 23:19-20 tells us they could charge foreigners interest, but not their brother Israelites. In other words, fellow Israelites could make loans to one another, but they were zero-interest loans. And verse 20 explains the reason: so that "the Lord your God may bless you in all that you undertake in the land that you are entering to take possession of it."

God said, "If you lend money to any of my people with you who is poor, you shall not be like a moneylender" (Exodus 22:25). God's people could lend money to their fellow Israelites without interest, and they could lend to a foreigner with interest, but they were not to get rich off of the poor by charging them a dime of interest.

By the way, all four Gospels tell the story of Jesus running the moneylenders out of the temple. They brought the nefarious business of moneylending, that is, cheating people and getting rich off of them, into God's house! And Jesus rebuked them, "You've turned my Father's house of prayer into a den of thieves" (Luke 19:46, paraphrased).

That wasn't God's plan and still isn't.

JESUS ENDORSED USING BANKS TO GAIN WEALTH

In the parable of the talents, Jesus told the wicked servant, "You ought to have invested my money with the bankers, and at my coming I should have received what was my own with interest" (Matthew 25:27). In order for a bank to pay interest to investors, it must charge interest to borrowers. Jesus endorsed that. If that was wrong to do, He would have never said the wicked servant should have at least put the money on deposit with the bank.

We should never attempt to get rich off of our family members or our church family. If you're in a business and all you see at church are potential customers and dollar signs from people you think you could make money off of, stay home. That's not why you go to church. No one should prey on church people or plot ways to get rich off God's people.

Also, if we have the means to help someone, we should give it to them or loan it to them without interest. You may be thinking, *I couldn't give money to anybody. I can't pay my own bills.* That's my point and that's our problem. We haven't been *following God's plan*, and that's why so many of us are in a jam – one which the devil helped create.

It was never God's plan for any of us to be in debt. If we had followed His plan and none of us was in debt, there would be no needy among us. We could help those who don't know Jesus, who don't know about God's plan, instead of having to take turns bailing each other out because we ignored God's plan and followed our own.

I know what I've just written sounds completely foreign to most people, but that just shows how far off of the road we've gotten. It should be normal among God's people that there are no needy among us (Acts 4:34). Why? Because we *follow God's plan* instead of following someone else's or coming up with our own.

ANY DEBT WE INCUR SHOULD BE SHORT-TERM

Here's what God told His people about debt: "At the end of every seven years you shall grant a release. And this is the manner of the release: every creditor shall release what he has lent to his neighbor. He shall not exact it [in other words, demand it] of his neighbor, his brother, because the Lord's release has been proclaimed" (Deuteronomy 15:1-2).

Moses was describing a canceling of all debts every seven years. Imagine that. In fact, in verses 9-11, it's clear those debts were permanently canceled, not just for the year of release.

I've heard some Bible teachers say that every seven years they gave people a year off so they could spend money on themselves and do their own thing and then, during the eighth year, they had to start paying again. That's not what the Bible teaches. Seven years was the limit.

Leviticus 25 talks about the year of jubilee. That was the year when basically everyone and everything got a whole year off. Nobody worked. Nobody did anything for an entire year. And it happened every 50 years. During the jubilee year, everyone would return to his family and his own property. All leased or mortgaged lands returned to their original owners. All slaves and laborers were freed. There was no sowing or reaping or gathering of grapes.

God instituted that. Every seven years, debts were canceled. Every 50 years, everybody got a whole year off. You're probably thinking, *Yahoo! Where do I sign up?*

How do we apply this today? Remember, this was God's teaching to the Jewish people. But there are applications for us.

Let's look at the seven years. I was reading an article in *USA Today* recently that said 31 percent of all car loans in America last for seven years.[19] I don't remember seven years being an option on my last car loan application. (By the way, the average monthly car payment in America these days is $554.)

I think the application for us is this: If we decide to go into debt for anything, it ought to be for the shortest possible amount of time. Because debt, instead of delivering your dreams, actually delays your dreams, and sometimes destroys your dreams.

I'll let you in on a secret that will help you. Every expenditure we make is a detour off the road to financial freedom. It doesn't matter what we purchase. Every expenditure is an exit off the road to financial freedom.

If you pay cash for a purchase or an expense, it's still a detour off the road, but the detour is not as disruptive as taking on debt. Pay cash, and you're able to get right back on the road. I had one of those slight detours not long ago. I had to spend $1,100 to replace the rocker arms on my car. (I didn't even know my car could rock!) And I didn't want to pay to replace them because I have other plans and goals for my money. I was discouraged about the expense; it bothered me the entire day. You know why? It was a detour. And even though I paid cash for the rocker arms and was able to get right back on the road, it put me further away from my dreams.

Expenditures and debt delay your dreams. They don't deliver them. So remember, if you go into debt, you take a detour off the road to financial freedom; and the larger the debt, the longer the detour.

IF WE GO INTO DEBT, WE NEED TO HAVE A PLAN TO PAY IT OFF

Psalm 37:21 says, "The wicked borrows but does not pay back." I've counseled a number of people over the years who wanted to file bankruptcy or who have filed bankruptcy. And they've all said the same thing, "The laws in America allow you to file bankruptcy and you can reorganize and start all over again." And I always respond, "Yes, but you still have to pay those debts."

"Why? Who said that?"

"God," I reply. And then I share that verse: "The wicked borrows and does not pay back."

Now if you want to use America's financial laws to reorganize and help get yourself back on your feet and pay all those people back, that's fine. But you cannot stiff your creditors. If you owe money to people, you should pay them.

Do you have any idea how many people and businesses over the years have been cheated by churchgoing people who claimed to be followers of Christ? That's wicked.

Jesus said, "For which of you, desiring to build a tower, does not first sit down and count the cost, whether he has enough to complete it? Otherwise, when he has laid a foundation and is not able to finish, all who see it begin to mock him, saying, 'This man began to build and was not able to finish'" (Luke 14:28-30).

If we cosigned for someone else's debt, Solomon warned in Proverbs 6:1, 4, we shouldn't even go to sleep before we get ourselves out of that mess. And he elaborated on that in Proverbs 22:27: "Why should your bed be taken from under you?" Most people don't think about that when they sign for a new car or a new home; they don't even dream that somehow, someway, something might be taken from them.

That's why Christian financial expert Larry Burkett said, "The first line of defense for your financial freedom is to pay your house off." Because, if your house is paid for, no one can come and take it from you. You'll always have a place to sleep and a roof over your head.

I've heard people say, "Yeah, but there's a tax deduction for this and . . ." Listen, anybody who makes financial decisions based on potential tax deductions is not thinking straight. Tax deductions come and go. We need to make our plans based on what God says, not what our accountant says.

Several financial advisors have told me I shouldn't be tithing. A tax accountant once asked me, "What's this *tith-eee* to your church for?" He pronounced it with a short "i" and long "e," like *pithy*. I explained to him it's pronounced *tithe* (long "i"; silent "e"), and it's a percentage we bring back to God each week. He replied, "Why in the world would you do that? You should invest that in the stock market." I told him, "No, you don't understand. If I didn't put God first, I wouldn't have anything I have. The tithe is not up for debate or discussion. It's a done deal because Jesus is Lord. End of discussion."

DEBT IS A SERIOUS OBLIGATION AND WE ARE OBLIGATED TO PAY IT OFF

We should take debt seriously and pay it off because we belong to God. We're Christians and Christians keep their word. Jesus said, "Let what you say be simply 'Yes' or 'No'" (Matthew 5:37). We need to learn to say no to debt and yes to *following God's plan.*

Let me tell you about one of my colossal failures. Twenty-plus years ago, a friend in our church was writing a business book and wanted me to write a fictional story for it. My friend gave me some ideas and I went to work. I wrote the first chapter and gave it to him and he liked it. His wife liked it, my wife liked it, and my kids liked it. I thought, *This isn't hard to do.* So I crafted this story and wrote all the chapters and my friend gave me a $2,500 advance.

He was a successful consultant with some 80,000 business contacts. He already had an editor and publisher in New York who were ready to go. He told me the potential of this book was amazing.

So, we both got excited and I bought a new car.

I told you earlier, the average monthly car payment in America today is $554. My monthly payment, more than 20 years ago, was $525. But I figured, *What's a few months of payments? That book's going to hit it big.*

We'll be gazillionaires. It's going to be amazing. Not a problem.

I don't know what happened, but the book never got published.

I learned an incredible lesson from that experience, and I'm praying you will learn this lesson the easy way by seeing how I learned it – the hard way. Here's the lesson: *Don't cash checks you don't have.*

I bought another car many years ago in Florida. As God is my witness, the salesman's name was Hank Williams Jr. He couldn't sing, but he gave me a song. He said, "Listen, you buy this car." It was a really small Toyota called a Starlet. They don't make them anymore (and I don't think they'll admit they ever did).

"You know what?" Hank said. "You're going to come back in here in a few months and you're going to be flush with cash and you're going to buy that brand-new Supra." He pointed to a slick, black sports car loaded with every bell and whistle you can imagine. And he said, "So start with this Starlet and in no time you'll be driving that Supra." It didn't happen. He gave me a song and I bought that car. But he was wrong.

Don't cash checks you don't have. Don't let other people talk you into going into debt based on some fantasy that your ship is going to come in or that a rich uncle you don't know is going to leave you a ridiculously large inheritance.

Instead, stick to the plan – God's plan.

OUR GOAL SHOULD BE TO BECOME DEBT FREE

Every one of us should have this goal: become debt free and stay that way for the rest of our lives. The Bible says, "Owe no one anything, except to love each other, for the one who loves another has fulfilled the law" (Romans 13:8).

Imagine for a moment what it would be like if you had no debts whatsoever – no car payments, mortgage payments, student loan payments, or any other payments. Your life would be changed forever. Freedom comes when you don't owe anything to anyone.

Our family has been debt free since November 15, 2001, and I have to tell you, our family is different than most families. Several years ago, Janis and I decided we no longer have to say no to anything. If God tells us to do something, we say, "Yes, Sir."

During all those years we were in debt, we had to say no. We couldn't help people we genuinely wanted to help. We couldn't do things we really wanted to do. We couldn't do things God had challenged us to do because we weren't *following His plan*.

My goal is to help everyone I can become completely debt free. Why? The bottom line is, freedom comes when you're debt free. That's why I want to help you get to the place where you don't owe anything to anyone.

That's why Jesus came to earth. It's the reason He died on the cross. You and I had a debt called *sin* we could never repay. We couldn't pay for it with our words or our works or all of our wealth. We could never pay that debt. And Jesus said to the Father, "I'll go pay that debt for them." The Bible says, "For our sake he made him to be sin who knew no sin, so that in him we might become the righteousness of God" (2 Corinthians 5:21).

Jesus did that so we could be debt free when it comes to sin. And friend, all I want to say to you is this: If you're not a Christian, if you haven't accepted Jesus Christ as Lord and Savior, that's one debt you can take care of today. Because Jesus has already paid your sin debt. Confess Him as Lord and believe in your heart that God raised Him from the dead (Romans 10:9-10). Once you have Jesus as Lord and Savior of your life, He'll help you with the rest of your life, and He'll help you with the rest of your debts.

Here's the bottom line. If we want to get on the road to financial freedom and stay there the rest of our lives, we need to *honor the Lord, follow God's plan, feed the pig, be faithful, bring the tithe*, and *avoid the detours*.

- Taking detours from God's plan for our lives and our finances can have disastrous results.

- Debt, rather than delivering your dreams, actually delays them and sometimes destroys them.

- Debt was never God's plan for His people.

- The Bible doesn't forbid debt, but it does discourage it.

- Jesus endorsed using banks to gain wealth.

- Any debt we incur should be short-term and we should have a plan to pay it off.

- Debt is a serious obligation and we are obligated to pay it off.

- Our goal should be to become debt free and stay that way our entire lives.

DID YOU KNOW...
"The first key that turned on a car's ignition arrived in 1949. Chrysler introduced it. Before that, cars required the push of a button to engage the starter."

(Source: https://www.caranddriver.com/news/a14499282/
the-evolution-of-car-keys-is-more-interesting-than-you-think/)

Most of us would like a smaller
stomach and a bigger bank account.
So why do we eat like there's
no tomorrow and spend
like government contractors?

BLC

7

SPEED LIMITS

In 2003, the same network that brought us *The Simple Life, Cops, Temptation Island,* and *American Idol* brought us *Joe Millionaire.* The series was an instant ratings hit for Fox. The unscripted show sent 20 women to a European country for a whirlwind romance with a man they thought was a dashing millionaire. In reality – it was a reality show, after all – "Joe Millionaire" was a blue-collar construction worker from Virginia with very limited financial security.

The women traveled to France for the opportunity to win Joe's affections. And Joe – real name Evan Marriott (no relation to the Marriott family with all of the hotels) – went to France to find the person with whom he'd like to spend the rest of his life, knowing that after making his choice, he would have to reveal to her and the whole world the truth about this monthlong masquerade and his limited financial standing.

According to the *New York Times*, the final episode was the most watched entertainment show to that point in the history of the Fox network; only the Super Bowl had a higher rating for the network that year.

The night of the final episode, there was a one-hour reunion of all the rejected contestants; it was viewed by 29 million people. That was followed by Joe's selection episode, watched by more than 40 million people. In it, the whole world learned Joe's choice was Zora Andrich, a substitute teacher. He also revealed he wasn't heir to a $50 million fortune but was actually a construction worker who made $19,000 the previous year.

To her credit, when she finally heard the truth, Andrich initially appeared to be good with it. She even expressed a desire to continue the relationship, and that was supposed to be the end of the show. But, in a surprise twist, the show ended by giving Joe Millionaire (Evan Marriott) and Zora Andrich a $1 million check to split between them.

Not long after that, they split as well.

It reminds me of what Solomon said, "Do not wear yourself out to get rich; do not trust your own cleverness" (Proverbs 23:4, *NIV*).

The only one who got rich from that show was the Fox network. Joe Millionaire isn't. And I'm pretty sure the woman he chose isn't either. One news reporter said she was a foster mom and divided her time between family, teaching yoga, and animal advocacy.

Every one of us has, at one time or another – some of us many times – played that same game. We've all tried to keep up with the Joneses or the Joe Millionaires and have gotten involved in the game – chasing a charade, a mirage, or an illusion.

We spend money we don't have on things we don't need trying to impress people we don't know or like, mortgaging a future we won't be able to enjoy because of a past we'd like to forget.

It's a game we can't win.

Solomon warned, "Those who work their land will have abundant food, but those who chase fantasies will have their fill of poverty" (Proverbs 28:19, *NIV*). Yet, when the next get-rich-quick scheme comes along, far too often we're mesmerized by it. We get caught up in the promise of fast cash, little effort, and all kinds of other make-believe fantasies that cause people to go crazy and do crazy things (like buying the "get rich quick" starter kit, attending meetings, buying books, CDs, DVDs, etc.).

All roads have speed limits that are in place to protect you, not to restrict you. The road to financial freedom has speed limits, as well.

The Bible says, "Wealth gained hastily [rapidly] will dwindle, but whoever gathers little by little will increase it" (Proverbs 13:11).

A lot of people falsely assume it will be different for them. They'll win big and quick, and after that, they'll be on easy street. Why do you think people go to casinos? Or sign up for the Publishers Clearing House Sweepstakes? Or stand in line at a gas station to buy lottery tickets? They're hoping to win it all, and they're hoping to win it all at once.

They're caught up in the game.

Jesus made an eye-opening statement in Luke 12:15: "Be on your guard against all covetousness, for one's life does not consist in the abundance of his possessions." He followed that with one of the greatest, most sobering, and shortest parables He ever told:

> The land of a rich man produced plentifully, and he thought to himself, "What shall I do, for I have nowhere to store my crops?" And he said, "I will do this: I will tear down my barns and build larger ones, and there I will store all my grain and my goods. And I will say to my soul, 'Soul, you have ample goods laid up for many years; relax, eat, drink, be merry.'" But God said to him, "Fool! This night your soul is required of you, and the things you have prepared, whose will they be?" So is the one who lays up treasure for himself and is not rich toward God (Luke 12:16-21).

The man in Jesus' parable wasn't just rich. He was very rich. He'd just experienced a bumper harvest. He'd never had a harvest like it before, but that created a problem. What would he do with the surplus? The ground God had given him produced a God-sized harvest. That's how it always happens. The harvest always comes from God, not from our hands or hard work.

I heard about an old, rundown farm. It had gone years without an owner. No real estate agent wanted to list it. It was in severe disrepair, overgrown with weeds. Fences were broken, nearly gone. There were holes in the roof of the barn. Most of the windows were broken. You couldn't even recognize the fields, which had produced years of bumper crops in the past.

A man eventually came along and bought the old farm. He spent several months and several thousand dollars fixing up the place. One day, one of his friends came by to say hello. He got out of his truck, walked over to the farmer and said, "Joe, this place looks wonderful. You and God have really done a great job here." Joe removed his hat, scratched his head, and said, "You should have seen this place when God had it all to himself."

There are a lot of people who think like that and live like that.

The rich fool did what so many other foolish people have done. He started thinking the harvest was a result of his own efforts, and worse, that it all belonged to him.

Here's the problem:

First, the harvest came from Heaven, not in response to his hands or hard work.

Second, the harvest wasn't all *about* him, nor was it all *for* him.

Third, God was no longer in the picture for the rich fool. The man was rich, but his swelling riches and recent successes had crowded out the very *source* of his blessings.

I've met a lot of people like the rich fool over the years. They pray and beg God for His blessings. But when the blessings come, they say, "God, butt out. I don't need You anymore."

Back to the story. It didn't take the rich fool long to make up his mind. He'd build bigger barns to store all the grain until the price went up. He'd sell the surplus and make even more money. Then he could relax, eat, drink, and be merry (v. 19). He was going to quit work, enjoy all he had accumulated, and probably enjoy an early retirement.

"I would paraphrase the story in today's terms like this," Chuck Swindoll wrote.

> "The business of a wealthy entrepreneur was off the chart. Every idea worked. Every decision succeeded. He added new accounts each month and the money rolled in. He began thinking, *This is a gold mine. My major problem is out-of-control growth. I'm running out of space. There seems to be no end in sight. This is my plan. I'll enlarge headquarters and I'll multiply my staff. I will add a warehouse nearby and open several branches each year for the next ten years, exactly as my consultant has suggested. As the business continues to grow, I will slip further and further out of the picture and leave the work in the hands of my efficient executive staff, and I will just take the profits and enjoy them. I might even retire early!*"[20]

But then came the shocker: "But God said . . ."

You'd better pay attention and live your life by what God says or the day will come when you are stopped dead in your tracks by what God says. That's what happened to the rich fool. God said to him, "Fool! This night your soul is required of you, and the things you have prepared, whose will they be?" (Luke 12:20).

That's the materialist's worst nightmare – somebody else ends up getting it all. But that's what was happening to the rich fool. It's insane to

105

make all your plans and spend all your money without any thought of God whatsoever.

"You ought to say, 'If the Lord wills, we will live and do this or that'" (James 4:15).

The application of the parable is found in that final verse: "This is how it will be with whoever stores up things for themselves but is not rich toward God" (Luke 12:21, *NIV*).

Then Jesus encourages us not to worry about anything (vv. 22-30), to put God and His kingdom first (vv. 31-32), and to lay up treasure in Heaven (v. 33). He concludes with this statement, "For where your treasure is, there your heart will be also" (v. 34).

The rich fool made at least three major mistakes:

First, he thought his bank account was more important than his Bible. The rich fool measured his worth by business deals, balance sheets, and bottom lines. The Bible didn't even enter the calculation. He probably saw himself as a self-made man. (By the way, a self-made man is always made of inferior material.)

He didn't think of himself as being self-serving, self-absorbed, or selfish. But listen to what he says: "*My* barns and *my* grain and *my* goods." My, my, my – was he ever off the road!

I want to be clear. The rich fool's problem wasn't his success. The problem was his stewardship (or lack thereof) of his success. Don't miss this: God is not against our success. He's the source of it. Deuteronomy 8:18 says, "Remember the Lord your God, for it is he who gives you the ability to produce wealth, and so confirms his covenant" (*NIV*).

Second, he thought his body was more important than his soul. What use does a soul have for barns, banquets, and beer? The soul has no interest in that stuff whatsoever. Those things have to do with the physical, material side of life. The soul is engineered for the spiritual side of life. The soul needs to be saved. The soul needs to be sanctified. The soul needs to be fed from the Bible.

That's why we feel good after attending a church service. When we sit under the teaching and preaching of the Word of God, it's fulfilling. There's something enriching about it. The opposite is true when we skip meeting together. We experience an emptiness when we stay away from church.

That's why when young couples have kids, something stirs in their hearts and they start finding their way back to church. That's also why middle-aged folks, when their kids turn away from God, start finding their way back to church. That's why successful couples, when everything implodes and goes bad in their lives, suddenly find time for church.

Why in the world would anyone want to skip or eliminate church from their lives in the first place?

Some people stay away from church completely until somebody dies. Then they have to go to a funeral and something stirs within them. They hear music during that service that brings a tear to their eyes. They hear Scripture and say to themselves, *I remember this.* Suddenly, they remember what they ought to be doing and where they ought to be on the Lord's Day. But, in too many cases, they leave the funeral wiping away the tears *and* the experience and don't return.

We live in a world full of fools who think the material is more important than the spiritual. Don't make that mistake. The rich fool did. But it wasn't his only mistake.

Third, he thought the temporal was more important than the eternal. The rich fool said, "I will say to my soul, 'You have ample goods laid up for many years. Time to party!'" I like what Bible scholar and author John Phillips said: "He was evidently still a young man. He assured himself that he had 'many years,' but he was going to be dead before daybreak."[21]

Dead before daybreak. Sobering isn't it? What would happen if that statement applied to you? "You're going to be dead before daybreak." Would that change anything in your life? Would that change your schedule? Your plans, priorities, pursuits? *You've got just a few hours left.*

I have an app from American Airlines that shows me how much time is left before a plane begins boarding passengers. On days I'm flying, that little app and that little clock drives everything I do. I've got to pay attention to it.

Most people, unfortunately, aren't paying attention. They go through life as if they are going to live forever. They never think about the possibility of being dead before daybreak or what would happen if they were.

Most people don't think about dying or being dead. We don't even like to talk about it, though the reality of death is all around us. People die every day. A funeral procession drives through our community every day. Sometimes several of them. But that's somebody else's problem, right? That's their family. That's their situation. That's not going to happen to us. Or so we think. We live in a world full of fools who have no idea how limited our time really is.

I've said this for years: I don't want my last meal to be airplane food. And I can't conceive of being in a box. I am so claustrophobic. I don't want to be lying in bed thinking, *They're going to put me in a box in the ground.*

Cremation? No. The whole thing mortifies me.

My mentor, Wayne Smith, and I used to talk about death. He would ask, "How do you want to die?"

"Well, first of all I don't want to. Let's start there."

"Me too."

As a matter of fact, Wayne would regularly say to me, "Barry, I want to go to Heaven, I just don't want to go tonight."

I would tell him, "I just want to go to sleep in bed and wake up in

Heaven."

A friend said to me, "Isn't the rapture a better way to do it?" I said, "I'll take that. That would be wonderful."

Here's the reality: None of us knows how much time we have. That's why John Phillips said of the rich fool: "He assured himself that he had 'many years,' but he was going to be dead before daybreak. Even as he was gloating over his fortune and his future full of fun and frolics, looking again and again at his bankbook and his balance sheet, the voice of God rang forth. God had been looking at the balance sheet that *He* was keeping of this man's life."[22]

God is keeping a balance sheet for all of us.

Phillips said God wrote one word on the rich fool's balance sheet, "Bankrupt!" And He said, "You fool." And remember how Jesus concluded this short parable: "So is the one who lays up treasure for himself and is not rich toward God" (Luke 12:21).

"When you're blessed with much, give generously," Chuck Swindoll wrote. "When you plan for the future, think terminally. . . . Whether you have much or little, hold it loosely."[23]

When I was a young preacher, I used to have 10-year and 20-year plans. When I develop a preaching schedule these days, it's for six months. And I think that is even a little presumptuous. You learn as you get older.

"Everything you have belongs to God," Swindoll continues. "He owns it all. If you maintain that perspective, then your grip on things automatically loosens. Moreover, you begin to discover that God doesn't care how much you have, whether a little or a lot; He simply wants your unquestioned devotion to Him above all, and He wants you to use what He has given you for His kingdom."[24]

Every golfer knows if you want to hit the ball farther, you have to loosen your grip on the club. I don't get to golf every day but would if I could.

(If you don't play golf, you have no idea how close to Heaven it really is. There's nothing better than standing at the tee of a par-5 hole and grabbing a driver with the intention of knocking the tar out of the ball.)

I have this tendency when I'm standing in the tee box with my driver. Everything inside of me says, *Grab the club harder and swing harder.* But that's not the way to make the ball go farther. The key to a long drive is actually to loosen your grip. And the few times when I remember to do that, the ball travels a lot farther.

So it is with material things. Everything within us tells us to grab all of our stuff and tighten our grip on it all. But that's not the key to a long drive on the road to financial freedom. The key is to loosen our grip.

Here are five quick observations.

DON'T TRY TO KEEP UP WITH THE JONESES OR JOE MILLIONAIRES

Stay in step with the Spirit. Paul said, "But I say, walk by the Spirit, and you will not gratify the desires of the flesh. For the desires of the flesh are against the Spirit, and the desires of the Spirit are against the flesh, for these are opposed to each other, to keep you from doing the things you want to do" (Galatians 5:16-17).

When I've got my driver in my hands, everything inside me tells me grip it and rip it. But as I've said, the key to a long drive is to do the exact opposite.

The world says, "You need to get all you can, pile it up, save it up, and hang on to it because it's all about you and you need to look out for number one." But that's completely opposite of what we ought to be doing. A war is being waged against us by the world, the flesh, and the devil. That's why we've got to stay in step with the Spirit and do what *honors God.* Do what God says to do, what pleases Him, and *follow His plan.*

It's a mistake to think you have to have it now. Or you have to have it all at once. That's what gets a lot of people, especially young people, in trouble. Young couples in their first year of marriage often think they ought to have everything their parents have, or more. It's a colossal mistake. It took their parents years to get where they are. Now their children want to have it all in six months? The only way to do that is to go out and charge it all or borrow it all – go in debt for it all. That's one of the worst things you can do.

DON'T MAKE DUMB DECISIONS TRYING TO IMPRESS YOUR FRIENDS OR COLLEAGUES

I have a confession: Every dumb financial decision I've ever made was done to impress somebody else.

For example, I used to buy a new car and leave the sticker on the window. In my younger years, I wanted people to know I'd gotten a new car. I'm sure you've never driven down particular streets with a sticker in your window so certain people could see your new car. But I did.

Now when I get a new car, which I rarely do, I want that sticker off of the window before I even drive it off the lot. I don't want anybody to know.

I used to buy a new car every six months when Janis and I first got married. She never questioned me. She never said anything about it. She'd come home and say, "Where did that car come from?"

"I got a new one."

"Oh, okay."

No wonder she cried herself to sleep every night. I never put the two things together.

Sometimes we make dumb financial decisions just to impress *ourselves*. "I could get that $400 suit, but that $800 suit – I mean, that's me. It's got my name all over it."

Stop doing that. Make wise financial decisions. Not dumb ones to impress other people.

DON'T TRY TO GET WHAT EVERYONE ELSE GETS OR HAVE WHAT EVERYONE ELSE HAS

Talk about a bear trap waiting for you. Trying to get what everybody else gets or trying to have what everybody else has is nothing but a trap – a BIG ONE! The problem is, there will always be someone who owns something that you can't buy.

Instead, you need to memorize a little sentence that will save you from more heartache and heartbreak than you've ever dreamed. Here it is: "Good for them."

Don't get caught up in the mad dash for cash and catch the fatal disease called materialism. Materialism has ruined more marriages, more careers, more businesses, and more lives than almost anything I know.

That's why the Bible says, "Be on your guard against all covetousness, for one's life does not consist in the abundance of his possessions" (Luke 12:15).

The first of the Ten Commandments is, "You shall have no other gods before me" (v. 3). And the tenth commandment is, "You shall not covet your neighbor's house; you shall not covet your neighbor's wife, or his male servant, or his female servant, or his ox, or his donkey, or anything that is your neighbor's" (v. 17).

Of all the commandments, God spent more time elaborating on the tenth than all of the others. I think I know why. A lot of people get the first one. They don't have any other gods. At least they think they don't. God's first. Most people understand "do not steal." They get "do not kill." All of those are understandable. But when it comes to number 10, "Don't covet your neighbor's house, your neighbor's wife, or his male servant, or his female servant, or his ox, or his donkey, or anything that is your neighbor's," some people think, *That's not really a sin, is it?*

But it is. God said, "Don't covet anything your neighbor has." Obeying that commandment will keep you out of a lot a trouble.

DEVELOP A BUDGET THAT WILL ESTABLISH SPEED LIMITS FOR YOU

That's what a budget does – it establishes speed limits. A budget is simply telling your money where to go and what to do ahead of time. It's not about *restricting* you. It's about *protecting* you and your family. It's not just writing down your debts, although that's good to do and will motivate you when you see what you're up against in black and white.

If you're married, both of you need to see and know what your obligations are.

But a budget is more than just writing down your debts. It's also writing down your dreams. If you don't have a budget, your dreams won't come true. Your budget establishes speed limits so you don't ruin your family and your future in a futile race to try to keep up with someone else.

The 10/10/80 plan is a terrific place to start. The first 10 percent goes to God. That's where it all starts. We always want to *honor the Lord* first because it all comes from Him and belongs to Him. Then, 10 percent goes to ourselves (for savings), and the final 80 percent is to live on. The 10/10/80 plan is the best plan I know for anyone to get on the road to financial freedom and stay there.

But to get on that road and stay there, you also need some speed limits. If you don't, you're going to be tempted by the guy who speeds by you, and you're going to want to speed up and get behind him or pass him. If you allow yourself to get caught up in that race, you may pay a price you never dreamed. We all need speed limits.

DECIDE TO PUT GOD FIRST IN YOUR FINANCES

It all starts with putting God first. It's the foundational step. You have to make the decision, "God is going to be first in my life."

The point of the parable of the rich fool is for every one of us. Jesus said, "So is the one who lays up treasure for himself and is not rich toward God" (Luke 12:21). If we think it's all for us, if we think it's all about us, that God blesses us just so we can be blessed, we've missed the whole point.

In 1982, James W. Jackson wrote a book called *A Study in Christianomics: What'cha Gonna Do with What'cha Got?* I loved the title upon first sight, so I bought it and read it. It's a great book. And that's really the question, isn't it? "What'cha gonna do with what'cha got?"

Are you going to *honor the Lord, follow His plan, feed the pig, be faithful, bring the tithe,* and *owe no one anything*? Because, here's the bottom line: *It all belongs to God.*

The Bible says, "For we brought nothing into the world, and we cannot take anything out of the world" (1 Timothy 6:7).

Don't miss this: What you and I have, we have only for a few years here on earth, and then we have to give it all back. Our task for the few years we have on this earth, between our arrival date and departure date – which could be in the morning for some of us – is to be faithful stewards and managers of whatever God gives us. So the question is:

What'cha gonna do with what'cha got?

- Trying to get rich quick is not a smart financial plan.

- One of the more sobering parables in the Bible is the one about the rich fool.

- Don't ever think your bank account is more important than your Bible, your body more important than your soul, or the temporal more important that what's eternal.

- God is keeping a balance sheet for all of us.

- We need to loosen our grip on our stuff.

- Don't try to keep up with someone else or make decisions trying to impress anyone else.

- Don't try to get what everyone else gets or have what everyone else has.

- Set some speed limits for your finances with a budget.

- Make the decision to put God first.

DID YOU KNOW...

"Up until the early 2000s, the only way to know what was going on behind you in your car was to look at your mirrors or turn your head around. In 2002, Infiniti came out with the first backup camera on the new Q45. Backup cameras are now required by law for all new vehicles."

(Source: https://www.popularmechanics.com/cars/g2778/most-important-automotive-tech-milestones/)

It's simple! Give 10 percent to God first.
Spend less than you earn. Pay off all debt.
Save everything you can, and you
can achieve financial freedom.

BLC

8

GOD'S HOV LANE

In 1986, when Barry Minkow was 20 years old, the company he started four years earlier, ZZZZ Best, debuted on NASDAQ. By the time he was 21, Minkow's company, a California-based commercial carpet cleaning and restoration business, had grown to where his share alone was worth more than $100 million.

But, according to John Thornton, who tells Minkow's story in *Jesus' Terrible Financial Advice: Flipping the Tables on Peace, Prosperity, and the Pursuit of Happiness*, there was a problem: his company was largely a fraud. In fact, ZZZZ Best never restored one carpet. Instead, his employees spent much of their time faking it: faking customers, faking sales, faking bills. They even deceived one of the biggest audit firms in the world, going to such great lengths as to place printed signs in the fronts of downtown office buildings they were supposed to be servicing and bribing night guards to recognize them as they brought auditors in to inspect the carpet restorations they weren't actually doing.

Unfortunately, all things – good or bad, it seems – must come to an end, and Minkow's end included a lengthy trip to a U.S. penitentiary. While there, Minkow checked out Christianity. Admittedly, at first it was to get a lighter sentence, but later he read the Bible more seriously because he was amazed by God's grace. He knew he was a sinner and he knew he needed reform. While in prison, Minkow got a new start on life and even earned an online degree in Christian ministry. He became more than a model prisoner. He put his old skills at deception to good use, or rather, he used them for good. From prison, Minkow assisted the FBI with cases, proving that nobody can spot a fraud like a fraud.

Because of his service, Minkow was released early. And this time, he steered clear of the financial markets. In fact, he became the pastor of the Community Bible Church in San Diego. Twenty years after ZZZZ Best's implosion, Minkow, now 40, had a new life, new wife, new family, new calling, and he seemed to be making the most of his new opportunities. His church grew fivefold and he started a successful side practice helping to uncover financial fraud.

In 2010, however, Minkow made headlines again. It seems he began to use his exposés of corporate financial shenanigans to his own benefit, betting in the financial markets against those he accused. His return to federal prison – along with an imposed penalty of more than $500 million in restitution – serves as a spectacular reminder of the proverb, "As a dog returns to its vomit, so fools repeat their folly" (Proverbs 26:11, *NIV*).[25]

Nobody likes to be taken for a ride. But the truth is, a lot of people who claim to be Christians try to take God for a ride when it comes to finances. And the worst part? They think they're getting away with it. But they're not. Nobody takes God for a ride.

My question is, if we *fake* our way through life, why would we expect a *real* reward in eternity? That's why I want to get as many people as I possibly can on the road to financial freedom. You don't have to fake your way through life. No one does.

Instead of faking it, we've been learning how to *honor the Lord, follow*

His plan, be faithful, bring the tithe, owe no one anything, and *remember it all belongs to God*.

The goal is to get on the road to financial freedom and stay there for the rest of our lives. Once we do, we're going to discover God's HOV lane. You may be thinking, *I didn't even know God had an HOV lane*. He does and you're about to find out about it.

Major highways in many metropolitan areas have an HOV lane where you can go faster and quicker than the rest of the traffic. But there's one requirement. You have to take someone with you – HOV stands for "high-occupancy vehicle," after all. That's the way it is with God's HOV lane, too.

The road to financial freedom isn't all about us or even just about us. God says, "I will . . . pour out so much blessing that there will not be room enough to store it" (Malachi 3:10, *NIV*). God says He'll give us more than enough, more than we need. Why? Because it's not all about us. God wants us to bring others on the road to financial freedom.

Parents, you need to work with your kids to make sure they get on the road to financial freedom. Young people, you need to bring your friends; tell them, "You need to be doing what I'm doing." College students need to bring fellow college students. Singles need to bring other singles.

Married couples need to bring their mates. They may come reluctantly, scratching and screaming, but you need to bring them on the road to financial freedom anyway. Grandparents need to make sure their grandkids are on the road to financial freedom. Divorcees, who've been dealt a bad deal, need to find other divorcees who've been dealt a bad deal and say, "Come get on the road to financial freedom with me. It'll change your life forever."

Employers need to bring their employees. Employees need to bring their fellow workers. Everyone needs to bring someone on the road to financial freedom. That's how you get in God's HOV lane.

In Mark 12, Jesus introduces us to someone who was in God's HOV lane on the road to financial freedom. You never knew it before today, but you're about to see the amazing story of a lady who was on that road:

> And [Jesus] sat down opposite the treasury and watched the people putting money into the offering box. Many rich people put in large sums. And a poor widow came and put in two small copper coins, which make a penny. And he called his disciples to him and said to them, "Truly, I say to you, this poor widow has put in more than all those who are contributing to the offering box. For they all contributed out of their abundance, but she out of her poverty has put in everything she had, all she had to live on" (Mark 12:41-44).

This woman had a phenomenal and powerful testimony. I hope you do, too. I hope we all do. She wasn't faking it when it came to her finances. She was living it. What a contrast between this poor widow and the superficial scribes and phony Pharisees of Jesus' day.

I want you to notice several things about Jesus.

First, notice where He sat (v. 41).

These are Jesus' final moments in the temple before going to the cross, and He chose *the treasury* as the place for His final temple teaching. Think about that for a moment. He contrasts the phony goodness of the religious leaders with the genuine faithfulness of this poor widow.

"Tired of contention the Lord now left the porches and ascended the steps that led from 'the terrace' into the temple precincts," John Phillips wrote. "The treasury was located in the Court of the Women, which occupied a space of about two hundred square feet and was surrounded by a colonnade. Inside and against the wall were thirteen trumpet-shaped boxes. These 'trumpets' bore various inscriptions, designating to what purpose the various gifts were directed. Nine were for legal dues, temple taxes, and the like; four were for voluntary contributions."[26]

Because it was time for the Jewish feast called Passover, there would have been thousands of people in Jerusalem. The whole city would have been filled with worshippers and people coming and giving tremendous amounts of money.

So Jesus walked in the treasury and watched. The wealthy were coming in throwing money into the offering box by the handfuls. Some of the people were giving cheerfully. Others were giving grudgingly. Some were giving because they wanted to. Others because they thought they had to. Others were giving to be recognized that they were giving.

Not much has changed over the years. That still happens every week in every church in every city, town, village, and hamlet all over the world.

Jesus was on His way to the cross, where He would give everything He could give. But for now, He was sitting in the temple, opposite the treasury, watching what others were giving. I wonder what that was like. He knew what He would be giving and was watching what they were giving.

Did you know Jesus is interested in what we do with our money – the money He gives us? Did you know He watches what we put in the offering – or what we don't?

While watching the people and the offering box, Jesus noted the wealthy were putting in a lot. They should. Jesus said, "Everyone to whom much was given, of him much will be required" (Luke 12:48).

If God has blessed you and you have a large salary or you received a large inheritance, you should give large. Paul said we should give in accordance with our blessings (1 Corinthians 16:2). The reality is, everything we have comes from God. Everything we get is something He has given to us. Deuteronomy 8:18 says, "Remember the Lord your God, for it is *he* who gives you the ability to produce wealth, and so confirms his covenant" (*NIV,* emphasis added).

I want to challenge you to take the blessing test. Here's how you do it. Get a legal pad and a pen and walk around your house and write down everything you see that God had nothing to do with. Walk in every room of your house or wherever you live, looking at all of your possessions. Go in the garage or driveway and look at your car (or cars) and, as you evaluate everything you have, write down everything God had nothing to do with. It will help you understand the real Source of all your blessings.

Do you have any idea how many people live on God's earth, which none of them had anything to do with? Or eat God's food – which they had nothing to do with? How many people drink God's water, breathe God's air, and use the resources God put into the ground, but had nothing to do with any of these? How many people enjoy a body with a heart, lungs, eyes, ears, hands, feet, a brain, arteries, and blood vessels they had nothing to do with? Yet so many of these people never give a thing, or much of anything, to God because they somehow believe everything they have belongs to them.

We used to sing an old song that repeated this line: "Count your blessings, name them one by one." The final line, "And it will surprise you what the Lord has done."

You and I don't own a thing. None of it belongs to us, none of it came from us, and none of us can keep any of it. We're going to find that out when the day comes and we draw our last breath.

John Phillips said this about that widow,

> Little did she know whose eyes were watching her that
> day! Little did she know the Lord of Glory "sat over against
> the treasury" that day! Little did she know who had looked
> into her purse! Little did she know what joy she had brought

to the Savior – a ray of sunshine on a dark and gloomy day of
controversy, a glow in the gloom that was now gathering all
about Him on His way to the cross. Little did she know that
her gift that day would find its way into the Gospels, and that
for the next two thousand years her generosity would be talked
about and preached about to the very ends of the earth![27]

Ray Stedman says, "The religious performance among these scribes
and Pharisees had reached such an absurd state of affairs, Josephus tells us,
that some of the Pharisees, before they made their contribution to the great
collection box Jesus was watching here, actually summoned a trumpeter to
go before them to get everybody's attention."[28] Josephus was a secular Jewish
historian, and he was saying these religious people tried to call attention to
themselves before they gave so they'd be noticed by men.

That sort of fanfare ran counter to what Jesus said in the Sermon on the
Mount: "When you give to the needy, sound no trumpet before you, as the
hypocrites do in the synagogues and in the streets, that they may be praised
by others" (Matthew 6:2). Certain individuals wanted to be seen by men,
they wanted the affirmation of men, and Jesus said the recognition among
their contemporaries would be their reward.

Now consider Acts 5 – the story of Ananias and Sapphira. This couple
received the jaw-dropping praise of men for a gift they brought to the
church. But in two separate, but related, instances they faced the undeniable,
inescapable judgment of God and dropped dead in front of the apostles and
others in the church that day. Why? Because they were lying about what they
gave. They tried to give the impression they were giving way more than they
actually were.

So, Jesus watched this poor widow walk in, and He witnessed what she
did. He called His disciples over, pointed out what she had just done, and

talked about *what* she gave. Then He said, "This poor widow has put in more than all those who are contributing to the offering box" (Mark 12:43). On physical scales, that wasn't true. But God weighs things on a different set of scales.

Then Jesus talked about *how* she gave. He said, "She out of her poverty has put in everything she had, all she had to live on" (Mark 12:44).

That widow gave so much that the only way she could make it was if God provided for her. It didn't make sense. It required a huge step of faith, and yet, by faith she gave generously and put herself in a position where she would have to say, "God, I won't make it unless You provide for me."

Israel's greatest king, David, said, "I have been young, and now am old, yet I have not seen the righteous forsaken or his children begging for bread" (Psalm 37:25). God takes care of His children. Somehow, someway, God always takes care of us.

Author and pastor Oswald Smith said, "It's not how much of my money will I give to God, but how much of God's money will I keep for myself."

Warren Wiersbe said, "God measures our gifts not by the portion but by the proportion."

The Bible is clear we should give in accordance to our blessings. If everyone in the treasury that day had given like that poor widow, it would have been the greatest offering in the history of the world!

I wonder what would happen today if every person in every Bible-believing church gave in proportion to their blessings. It would be a spectacular offering. The Bible says that's how we are supposed to give all the time.

Theologian and pastor John Walvoord said, "Jesus used her [the widow's] example to teach His disciples the value God places on wholehearted commitment. Their own commitment to Jesus would soon be severely tested."[29]

"I have often wondered what she found when she arrived home penniless that day," John Phillips said. "Did the Lord send Judas with a gift? Just a few days earlier, the Lord had received Zacchaeus's pledge, 'Half of my goods I give to the poor' (Luke 19:8). Did the Lord touch the heart of that penitent publican and direct his steps to that poor widow's door? We shall never know. But one thing we can anticipate – great will be her reward in heaven."[30]

So many people are hesitant to trust God to meet their needs. The God who placed the sun in just the right spot in our solar system so it warms us, but doesn't incinerate us. The same God who put all the water on the earth in all the right places and right amounts. The Bible talks about how God is the One who sets the boundaries of the seas and the One who put the mountains and everything else in place. (See more in Psalms 74 and 104.) God's the One who did all that. Yet people live their lives as if there is no God and as if they don't have to do anything He says. What a mistake.

Here are four things to remember in God's HOV lane:

DON'T PUT ON AN ACT

"Fake it till you make it" might be a motto for some businesses and businesspeople. But that won't work in Christianity. If you're faking it, you're wasting your time and God's. Jesus isn't impressed with cheap theatrics. Hypocrisy has dire, even deadly consequences. You can't dress up disobedience or selfishness. It's foolishness and a waste of time. Don't put on an act.

I've been stunned to watch some people put on incredible shows. They deceive so many others who think, *Wow, they're so spiritual. They've really got their act together.* People have no idea it's all a fraud.

I recently went for my annual physical. In addition to a thorough examination by my doctor, a nurse drew blood and tests were conducted on the sample. The medical team also wanted me to have an EKG – an electrocardiogram – a test that checks for problems with the electrical activity of your heart.

Did you know there's a spiritual EKG, a way to know the condition of your heart spiritually? When's the last time you had a "spiritual checkup"? Did you know the best way to determine the spiritual condition of your heart is to look at your spiritual EKG? Everybody has one.

It's your giving record (or lack of one).

Here's a news flash: A number of people already know what your spiritual EKG is. The people who count money at your church know whether or not you give. The people who help prepare your taxes know what your spiritual EKG is. But the most important Person to know your spiritual EKG is Jesus. So don't put on an act. It's a waste of time.

GIVING ISN'T A MATTER OF HOW MUCH YOU GIVE, BUT RATHER HOW MUCH OF GOD'S MONEY YOU KEEP

Get this in your head and your heart. It's not a matter of how much you give, but how much of God's money you keep. The tithe is a great place to start, but a horrible place to stop.

I always recommend the 10/10/80 plan – 10 percent to God, 10 percent to savings, and 80 percent to live on. It's a phenomenal plan that will help anybody. But tithing's the starting line, not the finish line. If all we do is tithe, that's like going to a stunning new swimming pool and saying, "I bought brand-new towels, a brand-new swimsuit, and brand-new flip-flops, and I'm so excited to be at this awesome new pool." And after that, you go home and talk about how much fun it was to be at the swimming pool. But all the while, you never got into the pool. You never got wet. You never swam.

If all you're doing is tithing – and tithing is wonderful – you're stuck at the starting line. That's where we all begin, but we need to get all the way in; we need to move forward. That's where the joy is. That's where the

126

real rewards are. That's where the bountiful blessings come. The tithe is a great place to start but a horrible place to stop. Be a tither but learn to give generously beyond that and watch what happens.

FOCUS ON GIVING YOUR BEST, NOT THE MOST

Giving is not a matter of who gives the most, but if we have given our best. Stop trying to outgive each other. God simply wants each of us to give our best.

This widow walked into the treasury and gave her best. Jesus called His disciples and said, "Come here, guys! Look at this woman. Do you see what she did?" And then He told them to follow her example.

This widow didn't take her husband on the road to financial freedom. He was already dead. She apparently didn't take her children on the road to financial freedom. They aren't mentioned in Scripture. By her faithfulness and example, she took the Lord's disciples on the road to financial freedom! Jesus said, "Follow her. Be like her."

Who are you taking with you on the road to financial freedom? You can't get in the HOV lane unless at least one other person is with you.

Some people try to beat the HOV-lane system. They're the only person in their car, but traffic is backed up and they think, *I won't get caught.* So they sneak into the HOV lane and drive for a bit, but as soon as they can, they move back into the unrestricted lanes. Why? Because they know they don't belong there and they know the consequences.

Have you ever tried to beat God's HOV-lane system? You move over there and think, *This is great, and I'm making so much progress, and God's blessing me.* But the truth is, God doesn't bless disobedience. You can't "fake it till you make it!" You need to get out of that lane until you get somebody in the car with you, because God's HOV lane is only for people who take others with them – by their faithfulness and example.

COMPARE WITH CARE

Don't compare your giving with what the poor widow gave or what anybody else is giving. Compare your giving with what Jesus gave.

Jesus gave it all, for all of us, on the cross. What will we give in response? Whatever we do, remember, Jesus is watching. Every place we go, everything we do or don't do, promises we make and don't keep – Jesus is watching it all. That's not a threat or something that should upset us. It's a blessing.

I'm glad He's watching. You've probably had times when you thought, *I wonder if Jesus sees? I wonder if Jesus knows? I wonder if Jesus cares?* Yes, He does.

Here's something else you need to know: It's not about the money. It's not about what you and I give.

In Joshua 6, the Israelites were entering the promised land God was giving them – an incredible land of milk and honey. A land so phenomenal they wouldn't believe it when they saw it. But to take possession of the land of promise, they had to face some battles. The first battle the Israelites had to fight was against the city of Jericho – a huge, ominous city with walls so wide they would actually hold chariot races on them.

God said to His people, "I want you to take the city. But everything in that city is to be devoted to me." Everything. Think about that for a moment. It was the *first* city, the *first* battle, in the promised land. The Bible teaches the *first* things, the *firstfruits*, always belong to Him.

So God said, "I don't want you to take a thing from the city for yourselves. The gold and silver are to be put in the Lord's treasury, but everything else is to be burned." The story is found in Joshua 6 and 7.

One guy among the Israelites thought he could do his own thing. Nobody would know, and everything would be all right. God wouldn't see or know what he did, and he'd just follow his own plan. You might even say he thought he could "fake it 'till he could make it."

Under the cover of darkness, while no one was watching, that man, named Achan, took some gold, some silver, and a Babylonian robe. He hid it underneath his tent, buried in the dirt. Nobody would have ever known anything about it. But the next day the Israelites went to battle a little village called Ai. Now remember, they faced down the giant city of Jericho and won. But when they went up against this little village, they were soundly defeated.

When Ai defeated them, the Israelites immediately said, "This isn't the way it's supposed to be with God's people. We don't walk in defeat. Something's wrong." And they cried out to God, and God said, "There's sin in the camp. Somebody did what I told them *not* to do."

The Bible says the Israelites cast lots and went through the process of elimination and finally came to Achan and his clan. Achan finally said, "It was me, I didn't think anybody would miss this stuff. I knew what God said, but I didn't think it was that important." So they took Achan, his wife, kids, relatives, and his cattle to the Valley of Achor, and there, the Bible says, "They burned them with fire and stoned them with stones" (Joshua 7:25).

You may be thinking that seems harsh. It's not.

God was very gracious and clear when He said, "The first things belong to me," and He told them to burn everything. The first time I read this story I was impressed that God was showing the Israelites, "It's not the stuff I care about. Burn it. I don't need it or want it. I want you. I want your heart."

It's not our money God wants. He owns it all. It all belongs to Him. One of these days you and I are going to be facing our final moments on this earth. And when that day comes, we're going to realize we can't hang on to any of it any longer. We can't go grab any more of it or earn any more of it. And it will finally make sense: *It all belongs to God.*

I'm trying to get you to understand that *now*, before that day comes, so you can enjoy the things God gives us. The Bible says God has given us all things richly to enjoy (1 Timothy 6:17).

If we will remember *Jesus is watching* and do what's right, we'll enjoy everything more.

- The road to financial freedom isn't just about us. We should bring others with us.

- Jesus is interested in what we do with our money and watches us.

- God values wholehearted commitment.

- Don't fake it until you make it. Be real.

- Giving isn't a matter of how much we give, but rather how much of God's money we keep.

- We should focus on giving our best, not trying to give the most.

- We shouldn't compare our giving with what anyone else gives, except what Jesus gave.

- God has given us all things richly to enjoy.

DID YOU KNOW...

"In the future, cars' interiors will be much more flexible, some allowing customization of color, light, privacy, and layout at the touch of a button. Volvo's 360c concept car envisages a multi-functional space that can transform into a lounge, an office and even a bedroom. Sun visors will become a thing of the past, with smart glass allowing us to control the amount of entering daylight at the touch of a button."

(Source: http://theconversation.com/cars-will-change-more-in-the-next-decade-than-they-have-in-the-past-century-113585)

I've found when people aren't tithing,
most likely they're cheating God
in other areas of their lives, too.
(Matthew 6:21)

BLC

9

THE RIDE OF YOUR LIFE

Lisa Allen, 34, had started smoking when she was 16, according to her file. She also began drinking at an early age and had struggled with obesity most of her life. At one point, in her mid-20s, says Charles Duhigg, who told her story in the prologue of his book, *The Power of Habit,* collection agencies hounded her to recover more than $10,000 in personal debts. An old résumé listed her longest job as lasting less than a year.

The woman who sat in front of researchers that day, however, was lean and vibrant with a runner's physique. She looked a decade younger than the photos in her chart. In fact, she looked as if she could out-exercise anyone in the room. According to the most recent report in her file, Allen had no outstanding debts, didn't drink, and was in her 39th month at a graphic design firm.

"How long since your last cigarette?" a physician asked, starting down the list of questions Lisa answered every time she came to this laboratory outside of Bethesda, Maryland.

"Almost four years," she said, "and I've lost 60 pounds and run a marathon since then." She had also started work on a master's degree and bought a home. It had been an eventful stretch.

What happened?

Allen went on to tell them the story. "It started in Cairo." The vacation had been something of a rash decision, she explained. A few months earlier her husband had come home from work and announced he was in love with another woman and was leaving her. It took a while for Allen to process the betrayal and absorb the fact that she was actually getting a divorce.

On her first morning in Cairo, Allen woke at dawn. It was pitch black in her hotel room. Half blind and jet-lagged, she reached for a cigarette. She was so disoriented she didn't realize she was trying to light a pen, until she smelled the burning plastic. She had spent the past four months crying, binge eating, unable to sleep, and feeling ashamed, helpless, depressed, and angry all at once. Lying in bed, she broke down. "It was like this wave of sadness," she said. "I'd felt like everything I'd ever wanted had crumbled, and I couldn't even smoke right.

"And then I started thinking about my ex-husband, and how hard it would be to find another job when I got back, and how much I was going to hate it, and how unhealthy I felt all the time. I got up and I knocked over a water jug and it shattered on the floor, and I started crying even harder. I felt desperate, like I had to change something – at least one thing I could control."

She decided she needed a goal – something to work toward. So she decided she would come back to Egypt and trek through the desert, and she would give herself one year to prepare. She knew in order to do that, and to survive such an expedition, she'd have to make sacrifices. In particular, she would have to quit smoking.

That one small shift in Allen's perception that day in Cairo – the conviction that she had to give up smoking to accomplish her goal – touched off a series of changes that ultimately radiated out to every part of her life. Over the next six months, she replaced smoking with jogging, and that in turn changed how she ate, worked, slept, saved money, scheduled her workdays, planned for the future, and so on.[31]

One change in her life changed everything in her life.

The same thing is true on the road to financial freedom. One change, *honoring the Lord*, can change everything else.

How do we do that? The Bible is clear: "Honor the Lord with your wealth, with the firstfruits of all your crops; then your barns will be filled to overflowing, and your vats will brim over with new wine" (Proverbs 3:9-10, *NIV*). When we honor God with our wealth, He will overwhelm us with His blessing.

Max Lucado, in his book *Grace*, put it this way:

> He overflowed the table of the prodigal with a banquet, the vats at the wedding with wine, the boat of Peter with fish, twice. He healed all who sought health, taught all who wanted instruction, and saved all who accepted the gift of salvation.
>
> God "supplies seed to the sower and bread for food" (2 Corinthians 9:10, *NIV*). The Greek verb for "supplies" (*epichoregeo*) pulls back the curtain on God's generosity. It combines "dance" (*choros*) with the verb "to lead" (*hegeomai*). It literally means "to lead a dance." When God gives, He dances for joy. He strikes up the band and leads the giving parade. He loves to give.[32]

John 3:16 tells us, "For God so loved the world that he *gave* his only son" (emphasis added).

HOW TO HONOR THE LORD WITH MONEY

The Bible gives us at least six practical principles for *honoring the Lord* with money:

1. Earn it ethically. The Bible says, "The wages of the righteous is life, but the earnings of the wicked are sin and death" (Proverbs 10:16, *NIV*). God doesn't say, "Earn money any way you want. Whatever works. Hit the casinos, buy lottery tickets, get involved in a get-rich-quick scheme, find ways to take advantage of people – it doesn't matter, as long as you get rich." No, the Bible is clear there is only one way to earn money – ethically.

2. Save it consistently. "Dishonest money dwindles away, but whoever gathers money little by little makes it grow" (Proverbs 13:11, *NIV*). The discipline is more important than the amount. Once we master the discipline of saving, the amounts will take care of themselves and, over time, get bigger.

If we do what the Bible says when it comes to money, and save it consistently, little by little, God will make it grow.

3. Spend it wisely. "A good man leaves an inheritance to his children's children, but the sinner's wealth is laid up for the righteous" (Proverbs 13:22). Most people don't start thinking about leaving anything to anyone until it's time for them to leave this world. They wait until they're too old to do anything about it. Yet the Bible says it should be our plan from the beginning to manage our money – giving, saving, and spending – in such a way that honors God and leaves something significant for our children and our children's children.

When we manage our money with that in mind, we'll learn to give, save, and spend whatever God gives us wisely.

4. Tithe it enthusiastically. "Honor the Lord with your wealth and with *the firstfruits* of all your produce; then your barns will be filled with plenty, and your vats will be bursting with wine" (Proverbs 3:9-10, emphasis added).

We've already seen tithing is the starting point, not the finish line. I've already said the 10/10/80 plan is the best financial plan I know of for anyone to get started, and it begins with a tithe. The first 10 percent goes to God. According to Malachi 3:8-12, it's how we *get under the spout where all of God's blessings come out.*

But we shouldn't just tithe. We should tithe enthusiastically. Not because we ought to or have to. Rather, we should do it because we really want to, because we know what God is going to do. He's going to meet our needs and more, and He'll pour out so much blessing we won't have room enough for it. In other words, He's going to bless us abundantly because we tithe obediently.

Everyone should tithe. But don't do it reluctantly or grudgingly. Tithe enthusiastically and watch what God does.

5. Give it generously. This is above and beyond the tithe. Remember, the tithe is the starting line, not the finish line. Proverbs 11:24 says, "One gives freely, yet grows all the richer; another withholds what he should give, and only suffers want."

When you first read that, it doesn't make sense. But Jesus said something similar: "Give, and it will be given to you" (Luke 6:38). The Bible teaches what we give, we get back, and what we try to keep, we lose.

Solomon continues in Proverbs 11:25, "Whoever brings blessing will be enriched [or will be made rich], and one who waters will himself be watered." In other words, the person who refreshes others will himself be refreshed.

Tithing enthusiastically and giving generously doesn't sound like the way to achieve financial freedom, but it's the way the Bible says to do it.

6. Invest it for eternity. Solomon warns that "riches do not last forever" (Proverbs 27:24). That's why Jesus said to "use worldly wealth to gain friends for yourselves, so that when it is gone, you will be welcomed into eternal dwellings" (Luke 16:9, *NIV*). In other words, use your wealth to help people come to know Jesus as Lord and Savior. Then when your money is gone, one day they will welcome you into Heaven, thanking you for helping make it possible for them to be there.

We need to leverage the things God gives us to reach people for Him. We shouldn't store up for ourselves treasures on earth where they can rot or be taken from us. Instead, Jesus said, "lay up for yourselves treasures in heaven, where neither moth nor rust destroys and where thieves do not break in and steal" (Matthew 6:20, *NKJV*).

We need to have an eternal mind-set for the management of our money. Here's why: "For we brought nothing into the world, and we cannot take anything out of the world" (1 Timothy 6:7). We have only a short time on this earth to be managers of whatever God gives us, and we must make a choice: Manage it in a way that honors Him or do our own thing.

"There are two kinds of people," C.S. Lewis said. "Those who say to God, 'Thy will be done,' and those to whom God says, 'All right, then, have it your way.'"

HOW WE CAN LIVE ABUNDANTLY

If we're going to get on the road to financial freedom and stay there for the rest of our lives, here's a reminder of what it will take:

Honor the Lord. That one decision will change everything.

Follow God's plan. Whatever God says to do, we do it. The 10/10/80 plan is the place to start.

Feed the pig. We need to be savers, not spenders. If you're a parent, you need to teach your kids about money and how things work in the marketplace. Don't give them chores, give them jobs. Don't give them an allowance, give them a paycheck.

Be faithful. "Our level of trust actually determines our level of treasure."

Bring the tithe. We don't *give* the tithe, we *bring* the tithe. It's not ours to give. The tithe belongs to the Lord. Tithing is a great place to start, but a terrible place to stop.

Owe no one anything. Debt, rather than delivering our dreams, actually delays them and sometimes destroys them. Every expenditure we make is an exit off the road to financial freedom. If we pay cash, we're able to get right back on that road. If we go in debt for something, it's a longer detour. The larger the debt, the longer the detour.

It all belongs to God. The story of the rich fool in Luke 12 is a sobering warning to everyone who is tempted to think God's blessings belong to us. Jesus said God called the man a fool, and then He said, "So is the one who lays up treasure for himself but is not rich toward God."

Jesus is watching. Jesus told the story of the widow bringing her offering – two small copper coins – that barely added up to a penny. Yet, He encouraged His disciples to follow her example because she gave all she had.

In 1982, Larry Walters floated into the air from his home in San Pedro, California, using a rather unique flying machine: a lawn chair lifted by 42 helium-filled weather balloons. He took along a CB radio, parachute, beer, sandwiches, and a pellet pistol, figuring he could shoot the balloons one at a time when he was ready to land.

Walters assumed the balloons would lift him well into the air, but was caught off guard when the chair soared to more than 15,000 feet and drifted into controlled airspace near Los Angeles International Airport.

When he landed and was arrested by officers from the Long Beach Police Department, a reporter asked him why he did it. Walters reportedly said, "A man can't just sit around."[33]

That's true for you and me, too. We can't just sit around expecting financial freedom to show up at our front door. Balloons won't help you achieve financial freedom. But the Bible will if you do what it says.

We've already read Solomon's words: "One gives freely, yet grows all the richer; another withholds what he should give, and only suffers want. Whoever brings blessing will be enriched, and the one who waters will himself be watered" (Proverbs 11:24-25). God blesses us to meet our needs and to enable us to meet the needs of others.

Jesus talked about the life we're called to live: "I came so they can have real and eternal life, more and better life than they ever dreamed of" (John 10:10, *The Message*). That's the abundant life. It's one of the rewards of being on the road to financial freedom.

In Deuteronomy 28, God talks about the abundant life He wants all of His children to experience. He sums it up with these words, "Blessed shall you be when you come in, and blessed shall you be when you go out" (v. 6). Basically, wherever you go, whatever you do, you're blessed – abundantly blessed. That's how God wants all of us to live, not just so we can be blessed ourselves, but so we can be a blessing to Him and others.

THE BLESSINGS OF FINANCIAL FREEDOM

We can expect at least four blessings on the road to financial freedom:

The blessing of the Lord. Solomon said, "[The Lord's] blessing brings wealth, and he adds no trouble to it" (Proverbs 10:22, *World's English Bible*). Sounds too good to be true, right?

We've already looked at Malachi 3:10: "'Bring the whole tithe into the storehouse, that there may be food in my house. Test me in this,' says the Lord Almighty, 'and see if I will not throw open the floodgates of heaven and pour out so much blessing that there will not be room enough to store it'" (*NIV*). In the next verse, He says, "I will rebuke the devourer for you" (v. 11). The "devourer" is the devil. Another translation says, "I will prevent pests from devouring your crops, and the vines in your fields will not drop their fruit before it is ripe" (*NIV*). Essentially, God not only is promising supernatural provision for you, He is also promising supernatural protection for what you already have.

Have you ever read what God did for the Israelites when they were wandering in the desert for 40 years? He told them, "I have led you forty years in the wilderness. Your clothes have not worn out on you, and your sandals have not worn off your feet" (Deuteronomy 29:5). How was that possible? Can you imagine having shoes and clothes for you and your kids that last 40 years?

When God blesses us, He does things that sound too good to be true. That's just who He is. The Bible says He "richly provides us with everything to enjoy" (1 Timothy 6:17).

The blessings that will benefit others. Hold onto your seat. If you thought that last part was too good to be true, you won't believe this. The blessing of the Lord will not only affect *you*, but everyone around you. Think about that for a moment. People will be blessed just by being in your presence.

Not only does that sound too good to be true, it sounds crazy.

But it's true.

Remember the story of Joseph? He was one of the 12 sons of Jacob. One day his father told him to go into the fields and check on his brothers. When his older brothers saw him in the distance, they were jealous of Joseph and decided to kill him. The oldest brother, Reuben, begged them not to kill Joseph, but to put him in a cistern.

The brothers ripped the richly ornamented robe from Joseph's body – the coat their father, Jacob, had given him – and dropped Joseph in a cistern. As they were plotting, a group of slave traders came by. The brothers thought, *We don't have to kill him. We don't have to leave him for dead. We'll just sell him to these slave traders, get some money for him, and they'll take him to another country. We'll never have to see him again.*

The slave traders took Joseph to Egypt, and he wound up in the employment of Potiphar, the captain of the guard for Pharaoh.

While working for Potiphar, the Bible says, "The Lord was with Joseph so that he prospered, and he lived in the house of his Egyptian master. When his master saw that the Lord was with him and that the Lord gave him success in everything he did, Joseph found favor in his eyes and became his attendant. Potiphar put him in charge of his household, and he entrusted to his care everything he owned" (Genesis 39:2-4, *NIV*).

Potiphar was blessed because Joseph was there. What's more, eventually the entire nation of Egypt was blessed because Joseph was there.

Our blessings will benefit others. When you decide, "I'm going to get on the road to financial freedom and live according to God's principles," you will receive God's blessings, and other people will be blessed just because you're doing what God says to do.

The blessings that will enable us to bless others. The Bible says, "You will be enriched [made rich] in every way so that you can be generous on every occasion, and through us your generosity will result in thanksgiving to God" (2 Corinthians 9:11, *NIV*).

In 2 Corinthians 9, Paul was talking about a love offering for the poor saints in Jerusalem. Their church was suffering and their people were facing serious problems. They had no money. The church in Corinth heard about it and decided to bless the church in Jerusalem. They gave a love offering from their blessings to bless others.

An interesting footnote: The church in Jerusalem helped start the church in Corinth.

The blessings that will enable us to do whatever we want, whenever we want. Another word for that is *freedom*. There's freedom that comes from doing things God's way.

The first thing God did for Adam and Eve after He created them was bless them. Genesis 1:27 says, "So God created mankind in his own image, in the image of God he created them; male and female he created them" (*NIV*). Adam and Eve were free to do whatever they wanted. As long as they honored God, they were blessed.

God told Abraham, "I will bless those who bless you, and whoever curses you I will curse" (Genesis 12:3, *NIV*). That's still true today. You'd have to have your head in the sand not to see God's blessing on the nation of Israel.

Early in the New Testament, we see Jesus preach His first sermon, and He started that sermon with the promise of God's blessing. We call that promise the Beatitudes (Matthew 5:3-12).

If we want to enjoy the blessings on the road to financial freedom, we have to recognize who the King of the road is and honor Him with the best of what we have.

Psalm 84:11 says, "For the Lord God is a sun and shield; the Lord bestows favor and honor. No good thing does he withhold from those who walk uprightly." God wants to bless us, and if we do it His way, we're in for the ride of our lives.

YOUR FINANCIAL FREEDOM TO-DO LIST

Here are seven things you can do right now to get going on the road to financial freedom:

1. Put God first and become a faithful, generous giver. It sounds like two things, but it's actually one, for when you put God first, your faith and generosity will naturally increase. Proverbs 11:24-25 says, "One person gives freely, yet gains even more; another withholds unduly, but comes to poverty. A generous person will prosper; whoever refreshes others will be refreshed" (*NIV*). It sounds counterintuitive that giving more is the way to having more, but that's the way God works. He doesn't do things the way we do them (Isaiah 55:8).

2. Start using half as much of everything and you'll find it will last twice as long. Whether it's toothpaste, water, electricity, or deodorant, apply this principle to everything you have and everything you use, and you will have more money.

3. Get in the habit of turning stuff off. As I mentioned in the introduction, if something beeps, blinks, buzzes, hums, glows, lights up a room, provides music, broadcasts images, helps you brush your teeth, keeps your food fresh and your milk cold, vacuums the dirt off your floor, turns ordinary bread into toast, delivers a hot cup of coffee, etc., it's costing you money. No one needs five clocks to tell them what time it is; no family needs four TVs on at the same time, especially when no one is in the room. If you leave a room, turn everything off. If you leave the house, turn the thermostat down (especially if you are going to be gone all day); better yet, use the computerized settings on the thermostat to regulate energy use throughout the day.

4. Be aware Starbucks may be costing you big bucks. If you don't go there, it may be 7-Eleven, Panera Bread, Sonic, or someplace else. For me, it's Starbucks, and I can't get out of there without spending at least $5. If I do that five days a week, that's $1,300 a year! By cutting back and putting that

$5 into savings instead, I can put $1,300 away yearly for a rainy day or even a sunny one. By exercising some simple discipline, we can save significantly more than we ever dreamed.

5. Lunch is expanding your waistline and affecting your bottom line. When you figure the cost of your lunch, drink, and tip, it's hard to walk out of any restaurant without spending at least $10. If we do that five days a week, that's $2,600 a year.

When our family decided to rid ourselves of debt, I took a brown-bag lunch to work every day. Yes, I missed going to restaurants. No, the food wasn't as good, and yes, it got boring after a while. Yes, people made fun of me and thought I'd lost my mind. But it was one of the smartest things I've ever done. I eliminated going out to lunch and was able to pay off our debts that much faster.

6. Drink water. You'll drink less and save more. Paying $2.50 for a glass of tea or a soft drink is insane. The profit margin for restaurants is through the roof. Lots of times restaurants give away free chips or some other kind of salty appetizer just so people will order more drinks. Their target is usually the folks who drink alcohol, since the cost per drink is nearly double or triple that of other drinks. Drink water, but don't pay for bottled water or spring mountain water or whatever luxurious line they suggest to justify making you pay for it.

7. Stop going out until you have more money coming in than going out. It's almost impossible for two people to go to dinner and a movie for less than $75. That's $3,900 annually if you go to dinner and a movie every week. If you take your kids with you, you're going to spend more. If you leave them home with a sitter, you'll still spend more.

The goal is to earn more interest every day than you spend. You can do that. Anyone can. But to do that means you have to get out of debt and put some serious money into savings every week. I've just shown you where you can come up with an extra $8,000 to $10,000, and probably more. It's up to you to decide to get started and do it.

Start today and you'll be on your way. My prayer is that you'll get on the road to financial freedom and stay there the rest of your life!

Bottom line: We're blessed so we can bless God and others. As we keep blessing Him and others, His blessings will continue uninterrupted, and we will enjoy a freedom we never dreamed was possible.

Jim Henry, former pastor of the First Baptist Church of Orlando, Florida, shared this story:

In the early days of World War II, after Germany had captured France, the French people were in a strange situation. Part of their country was free and unoccupied by the enemy while much of it, including Paris, was occupied and controlled by the Nazis. To escape into free France became the goal of many people who lived in Paris, who'd been tormented daily by their captors.

Etta Shiber was an American living in Paris at the time of France's fall. Three years later she wrote a book titled *Paris Underground* to tell the world about life in Nazi-dominated France.

In a certain village near the border dividing free and Nazi-controlled France, the citizens began noticing some unusual goings on at a local church. There was a cemetery out back and every time there was a funeral, far more mourners went into the church than came out.

There was a good reason.

While the main door of the church lay in occupied France, far to the rear was an old forgotten door, which opened to unoccupied territory. The people walked into the church in bondage and walked out free.

I'm hoping the same thing happens with this book. Maybe you were dealing with the bondage of bills, burdens, debts, and discouragement when you began reading. My prayer is you will be different by the time you finish reading the next chapter and you will decide to do it God's way moving forward, not just with your finances, but in every area of your life.

I'm also praying you'll get on the road to financial freedom and stay there the rest of your life!

- One change in your life can change everything.

- When it comes to money we are to earn it ethically, save it consistently, spend it wisely, tithe it enthusiastically, give it generously and invest it for eternity.

- There are a number of blessings that will come to us, and even allow us to bless others, once we are on the road to financial freedom.

- Put God first and become a faithful, generous giver.

- Start using half as much of everything and it will last twice as long.

- Get in the habit of turning stuff off.

- Be aware Starbucks may be costing you big bucks.

- Lunch is expanding your waistline and affecting your bottom line.

- Drink water. It's cheaper and better for you.

- Stop going out until you have more money coming in than going out.

DID YOU KNOW...

"Just as Apple and Samsung have taken over a mobile phone market that Nokia and Blackberry once dominated, Tesla, Apple, Dyson, and Google could become the most recognized automotive brands of the future."

(Source: http://theconversation.com/cars-will-change-more-in-the-next-decade-than-they-have-in-the-past-century-113585)

While you're amassing your
personal stockpile of stuff,
remember you'll be judged
for what you did with
what God gave you.
(2 Corinithians 5:10)

BLC

10

A SECOND CHANCE

As a redshirt freshman at Texas A&M in November 2012, he skyrocketed into the national spotlight, leading the Aggies to a 29-24 upset of No. 1-ranked Alabama. The following month, he became the first freshman ever to win the Heisman Trophy. He broke a number of NCAA Division I Football Bowl Subdivision and Southeastern Conference records, including being the first freshman to pass for 3,000 yards and run for 1,000 yards in a single season.

Janis and I were at Cowboys Stadium in Arlington, Texas, on January 4, 2013, for the Cotton Bowl Classic, when Johnny Manziel led Texas A&M to a 41-13 victory over the Oklahoma Sooners. It was a miserable night for us Sooner fans, surrounded by thousands of Aggie fans. But it was also a magical night as we watched this freshman phenom, called "Johnny Football," run all over the field – no one could catch him.

During the season and into the postseason, after he would make a great play, Manziel would raise his hands in the air, rub his fingers together, as if to say, "MONEY!" He even went by the moniker "Money Manziel" when he signed autographs.

The Cleveland Browns traded up to select Manziel in the 2014 NFL

Draft, but it didn't work out the way most people, including the fleet-footed quarterback, thought it would. In an April 2016 article titled, "The Ballad of Johnny Football: How Manziel's Career Cratered," Jon Schuppe wrote, "Quarterback Johnny Manziel often seemed on the precipice of disaster, even when he was most brilliant.

"Brash, electric and unapologetic, Manziel was for a few years one of the greatest young football players in America, a fleet, improvisational quarterback who seemed to flourish under pressure. But he couldn't seem to find his off-switch, often appearing hellbent on destroying himself. He drank, fought, partied, talked smack, drove recklessly, went to rehab and still kept getting into trouble. . . .

"Two sports agents quit on him since February, when his father, Paul Manziel, told the *Dallas Morning News*: 'I truly believe if they can't get him help, he won't live to see his 24th birthday.'"[34]

What happened to Johnny Manziel? It once appeared he was on the road to a promising NFL career, but he took another road and, as of this writing, he's still hoping for a second chance.

MY FINANCIAL FREEDOM DO-OVERS

If you feel like Johnny Manziel when it comes to your finances and would like another shot at achieving financial freedom and seeing your dreams come true, what would you want to do? I'm pretty sure all of us would do some things (maybe a lot of things) differently if we got a do-over on life. Especially when it comes to our finances.

Looking back over my life, I can guarantee I would do some things differently. For example:

I would've started getting serious about saving a lot sooner. What I wouldn't give to have known then what I know now. It would have been just as easy – when I was mowing lawns in junior high or working as a janitor at an apartment complex in high school or at McDonald's during college – to save 10 percent of whatever I earned. But I didn't. I didn't save 5 percent. I didn't even save 1 percent. Every week I spent every cent I earned. I'd give anything to have a do-over on that.

I would've avoided debt like an Olympic athlete avoids the doughnut shop. I had no idea the hole I was digging when I repeatedly signed papers and piled up more debt than I could afford for things I didn't need. The commitment to pay additional interest, which I really didn't understand, meant I was paying a lot more with debt than I ever would've paid had I waited until I had the money. I shared in *The ABCs of Financial Freedom* that DEBT is a "Dumb Explanation for Buying Things." In reality, *debt* is you and me attempting to give ourselves what God hasn't given us yet. All these years later, I now understand it is far wiser to save the money up front and save ourselves from the heartache later.

I would've taken advantage of payroll deductions. Years ago, I didn't want anyone taking money out of my paycheck. I wanted it all, every dime of it, so I could spend every dime of it. How dumb was that? I wish I would've had $40 a week taken out of my paycheck to fully fund my IRA back in the 1980s when I first opened one. Instead, I paid the $40 whenever I had it, and most weeks – you guessed it – I didn't have it. I'd already spent it on stuff I thought I had to have.

I would've been more generous in my giving. I've tithed since elementary school and given beyond the tithe most of my life. But I could've and should've been far more generous in my giving than I've been. Again, the reason I didn't give more was because I'd already spent more than I had, a practice I continued every week for years. (I'm sure I'm not the only one who has done that.)

I would've had a plan for my finances and my future. I guess when you're young and think you'll live forever, you just aren't concerned about next week, next year, and so on. You live each day to the fullest, believing there will always be a tomorrow, you'll always have a job, and you'll never have any worries. But we don't know any of that. In fact, James 4:13-17 warns us we don't have the promise of tomorrow. Our lives are a mist. And, if we're honest, so is our money. Just like our lives, our money "appears for a little while and then vanishes" (v. 14, *NIV*).

I would have taught every member of my family God's principles for managing the money He gives us and also how things work in the marketplace. Every member of my family is doing terrific now, including my grandsons. But I could have made it so much easier for all of them if I had been following God's plan, putting His principles into practice, teaching them, and making sure they got it.

OUR FINANCIAL FREEDOM REALITY (OUR STRATEGY)

The reality is, we don't get a do-over on life or our finances. But one thing we *can* do is make changes to make sure we're correctly doing now what we should've been doing for years.

So what does that look like for me and my family?

I save as much as I can every week. I have the maximum amount deducted from my paycheck each week and so does my wife. It goes into our 403(b) accounts at The Solomon Foundation, the fastest-growing Christian financial institution in America, and one of the largest, based in Parker,

Colorado. (They pay the highest rates in the industry.) Then I have The Solomon Foundation take a fixed amount out of my bank account every week, via EFT (electronic funds transfer), and place it in an account, earning interest for our family. Whatever is left after our bills, I put into a savings account at the credit union where we do our local banking (see Proverbs 13:11).

I don't do debt anymore and haven't since 1999. We pay cash for everything. If we don't have the money, we don't buy it until we do. As I said before, it doesn't take any more discipline to save the money up front than it does to find the money to pay off a debt with interest later on (and it's much smarter, too! See Proverbs 13:18).

I take advantage of payroll deductions for saving and also use online bill paying and online giving. Technology is our friend when it comes to saving, bill paying, and giving. It makes those functions easy and automatic. I can't believe it took me so long to start. I wish I had done it years ago. What a blessing to make saving and giving automatic.

I try to be more generous every year – not only in our giving to our local church, where the majority of our giving goes every week and every year, but also in our day-to-day living. I've found the Bible promise is true that we "will be [made rich] in every way so that [we] can be generous on every occasion" (2 Corinthians 9:11, *NIV*). I've also discovered the more you give and the more generous you are, the more you have (see Proverbs 11:24-25).

I have a plan and a strategy to get there. We have a budget. We also have a plan that goes beyond our budget and a specific strategy to achieve that plan. That plan and strategy are the essence of this book. It's not a wish, dream, or even a goal. It's a defined plan that takes discipline and determination. Here's the good news: Anyone can do it. Everyone should do it and should be teaching it to every member of their family, passing it on to succeeding generations (see Proverbs 13:22).

START NOW!

So where are you today? If you could start over, what would you do? I'm pretty sure all of us would do some things – maybe a lot of things – differently if we got a do-over on life. Especially when it comes to our finances.

That's what Michael Vick did. Vick is one of the greatest athletes ever to play professional football. He played 13 seasons with the Atlanta Falcons, Philadelphia Eagles, New York Jets, and Pittsburgh Steelers. He used his remarkable running abilities to transform the quarterback position in the NFL.

He was named to three Pro Bowls, holds the record for most career rushing yards by a quarterback (6,109), and had the most rushing yards for any quarterback in a single season (1,039) until Lamar Jackson broke that record in 2019.

Unfortunately, most people know Michael Vick for being involved in an illegal dog-fighting ring. He bankrolled a dog-fighting operation, was sentenced to 23 months in prison, and wound up losing virtually everything he had.

Vick became a Christian in high school, but instead of *following God's plan*, he came up with his own. The more success he had on the football field, apparently the less he felt he needed God.

He earned millions of dollars as one of the top quarterbacks in the NFL, but lost it all and had to file Chapter 11 bankruptcy in 2008.

Former Indianapolis Colts head coach Tony Dungy went to see Vick during his final months in federal prison in Leavenworth, Kansas. Dungy encouraged Vick to get God back in his life and everything would work out.

In November 2017, Vick made the final $1.5 million payment to his creditors, meaning he paid back $17.4 million of the $17.6 million he owed when he filed bankruptcy in July 2008. The trustee involved in Vick's bankruptcy said, "Paying 99 cents on the dollar, which he did, is remarkable. It happens in, maybe, one out of 100 cases."

Vick said, "I didn't want to stiff people who never stiffed me."

That's a great story, and Michael Vick has a tremendous testimony. But what would his testimony be if he had kept God first in his life all along?

What could our testimony be?

Here's my recommendation: Don't wait, hoping for a do-over. Do the right things, right now. Keep doing them diligently, consistently, and enthusiastically, and watch what happens.

Remember two things: Stewardship doesn't have anything to do with what's in your bank account. It has everything to do with what's in your heart. And . . . when it comes to your financial freedom, you're the quarterback.

Get on the road to financial freedom today. Don't wait another minute and drive carefully – biblically, and take your family, your friends and as many people as you can.

- Don't wait for a do-over. Do what's right, right now.

- Honor the Lord.

- Follow God's plan.

- Feed the pig.

- Be faithful.

- Bring the tithe.

- Avoid the detours.

- Don't try to get what everyone else gets or have what everyone else has.

- Take someone with you.

- Enjoy the blessings and share them.

DID YOU KNOW...
"While the look and feel of our cars has changed
in the past 100 years, the way we drive them hasn't.
But fundamental change is coming. In the next decade,
not only will the way they're powered and wired
have shifted dramatically, but we won't be
the ones driving them anymore."

(Source: http://theconversation.com/cars-will-change-more-in-
the-next-decade-than-they-have-in-the-past-century-113585)

NOTES

Chapter 1: READY TO HIT THE ROAD?

1. Said-Moorehouse, Lauren, and Alla Eshchenko. "Chess Grandmaster, 20, Dies in Parkour Balcony Fall." *Edition.cnn.com* (November 28, 2016). https://www.edition.cnn.com/2016/11/28/sport/yuri-eliseev-chess-grandmaster-dies/.

Chapter 2: WHOSE ROAD IS IT ANYWAY?

2. Searcy, Nelson, and Jennifer Dykes Henson. *Maximize: How to Develop Extravagant Givers in Your Church*. Grand Rapids: Baker, 2010. 147.

3. Evans, Tony. *The Kingdom Agenda: What a Way to Live!* Chicago: Moody, 2006. 338.

Chapter 3: ON-RAMPS AND EXITS

4. *Vasa Museum.* https://www.vasamuseet.se/en. "Vasa Museum." *Wikipedia.com.* https://en.wikipedia.org/wiki/Vasa_Museum.

5. MacArthur, John. *The MacArthur New Testament Commentary*. Chicago: Moody, 1983.

6. Ibid.

Chapter 4: SIGNS, LINES, AND FINES

7. Associated Press. "Madoff Reportedly Cornered the Hot Chocolate Market in Prison." *Foxnews.com* (January 14, 2017). http://www.foxnews.com/us/2017/01/14/madoff-reportedly-cornered-hot-chocolate-market-in-prison.html.

8. "Will Madoff's Investors Break Even?" *Time.com* (December 2010). http://business. time.com/2010/12/07/will-madoffs-investors-break-even/.

9. "Bernie Madoff." *Wikipedia.com*. https://en.wikipedia.org/wiki/Bernard_Madoff. "Charity Caught Up in Wall Street Ponzi Scandal." *Foxnews.com* (December 13, 2008). http://www.foxnews.com/story/2008/12/13/charity-caught-up-in-wall-street-ponzi-scandal.html.

10. Warren, Richard. "5." *The Purpose Driven Life*. Cleveland: Findaway World, 2005. 46.

Chapter 5: GIVE ME THE KEYS

11. Bruillard, Karin. "Two Moose Locked Antlers in a Fight, Then Froze Together in a Stream." *The Washington Post* (November 17, 2016). https://www.washingtonpost.com/news/animalia/wp/2016/11/17/two-moose-locked-antlers-in-a-fight-then-froze-together-in-a-stream/.

12. Howard, Brian Clark. "Two Bull Moose Found Frozen in Mortal Combat." *National Geographic*. https://news.nationalgeographic.com/2016/11/two-moose-found-in-ice-antlers-locked-alaska-speeddesk/.

13. Batterson, Mark. *If: Trading Your If Only Regrets for God's What If Possibilities*. Grand Rapids: Baker, 2016. 152.

14. Ramsey, Dave. *How to Have More Than Enough*. New York: Penguin, 2000.

15. "Prestonwood Baptist Church." http://www.prestonwood.org/home.

16. "Discover." In Touch Ministries – Home. Website: https://www.intouch.org/.

Chapter 6: DETOUR AHEAD

17. Charles Swindoll has told this story in *Come Before Winter and Share My Hope* as well as his devotional, *Day by Day with Charles Swindoll*. Facts about Foster's life and death can be found at: "Stephen Foster Biography." Pitt.edu (June 6, 2012), www.pitt.edu/~amerimus/Fosterbiography.html; "Stephen Foster: 9 Facts on America's First Pop Artist." Biography.com (January 11, 2015), www.biography.com/news/stephen-foster-songs-facts; and Skirboll, Aaron, "The Next Page: Stephen Foster's Sad End." *Pittsburgh Post-Gazette* (March 1, 2014), http://www.post-gazette.com/opinion/Op-Ed/2014/03/02/Next-Page-Stephen-Foster-s-sad-end/stories/201403020083.

18. Ramsey, Dave. *The Total Money Makeover: A Proven Plan for Financial Fitness*. Nashville: Nelson, 2013.

Chapter 7: SPEED LIMITS

19. Tompor, Susan. "How Much Is Too Much for a Car Payment?" *USA Today* (January 23, 2017).

20. Swindoll, Charles R. *Swindoll's New Testament Insights*. Grand Rapids: Zondervan, 2010. 329.

21. Phillips, John. *Exploring the Gospel of Luke: An Expository Commentary*. Grand Rapids: Kregel Publications, 2005. 181.

22. Ibid.

23. Swindoll. *New Testament Insights*. 329.

24. Ibid., 334.

Chapter 8: GOD'S HOV LANE

25. Thornton, John, *Jesus' Terrible Financial Advice: Flipping the Tables on Peace, Prosperity, and the Pursuit of Happiness*. Chicago: Moody, 2017. 146-147.

Parlow, Roger. "Barry Minkow: All-American Con Man." *Fortune* (January 5, 2012). http://fortune.com/2012/01/05/barry-minkow-all-american-con-man/.

"Barry Minkow." *Wikipedia.com*. https://en.wikipedia.org/wiki/Barry_Minkow.

26. Phillips, John. *Exploring the Gospel of Mark: An Expository Commentary*. Grand Rapids: Kregel Publications, 2004. 265.

27. Ibid., 266.

28. Stedman, Ray C. and Jim Denney. *The Ruler Who Serves*. Grand Rapids: Discovery House, 2002. 130.

29. Walvoord, John F., and Roy B. Zuck. *The Bible Knowledge Commentary: An Exposition of the Scriptures*. Colorado Springs: Victor, 2004. 166.

30. Ibid., 266.

Chapter 9: THE RIDE OF YOUR LIFE

31. Duhigg, Charles. *The Power of Habit*. New York: Random House, 2014. xi-xiv.

32. Lucado, Max, and Amanda Haley. *Grace: More Than We Deserve, Greater Than We Imagine*. Nashville: Thomas Nelson, 2012. 109.

33. Long, Tony. "July 2, 1982: Up, Up and Away With 42 Balloons." *Wired.com* (July 2, 2009). www.wired.com/2009/07/dayintech_0702/.

Chapter 10: A SECOND CHANCE

34. Schuppe, Jon. "The Ballad of Johnny Football: How Manziel's Career Cratered." *NBCNews.com* (April 26, 2016). https://www.nbcnews.com/news/sports/ballad-johnny-football-how-manziel-s-career-cratered-n562636.

35. Cockes, Timothy. "In Prison, NFL Star Michael Vick Returned to Faith." *Baptist Press* (January 31, 2018). http://www.bpnews.net/50283/in-prison-nfl-star-michasel-vick-returned-to-faith.

36. Farmer, Sam. "Tony Dungy's Work with Michael Vick Is Laudable." *Los Angeles Times* (August 16, 2009). http://articles.latimes.com/2009/aug/16/sports/sp-nfl-farmer16.

37. Stricklin, Art. "Michael Vick Shares First-Ever Testimony." *Baptist Press* (February 8, 2010). http://www.bpnews.net/32239.

TO CONTACT THE AUTHOR

Barry L. Cameron, Senior Pastor
Crossroads Christian Church
6450 S. State Highway 360
Grand Prairie, TX 75052

or

http://www.crossroadschristian.org

TO READ BARRY'S BLOG EACH WEEK:

http://www.crossroadschristian.org/blog/

FOLLOW BARRY ON

f barry.cameron.399

🐦 @BarryLCameron

📷 @BarryLCameron

in linkedin.com/pub/barry-cameron/32/538/6aa

BONUS BLOGS

PLAY NOW, PAY LATER

By Barry Cameron, September 27, 2019

The headline was, **Millennials: Go ahead and take that vacation instead of paying off your student debt.** And the opening line of the USA TODAY article was even more shocking. Here's what it said: "After saving up for her honeymoon, financial author Erin Lowry chose to use it for her honeymoon, rather than pay off her husband's student debt." [1]

Proverbs 24:27 says, "Prepare your work outside; get everything ready for yourself in the field, and after that build your house." In other words, do what you *have* to do first, then you can do whatever you *want* to do.

But that goes against the failed philosophy of "if it feels good do it. Who cares what it costs?" We all should. Truth is debt delays our dreams instead of delivering them and in some cases destroys them. Why? Again, Proverbs 22:7 warns, "The rich rules over the poor, and the borrower is the slave of the lender."

She went on to say, "To some people, our choice might seem extravagant." [3]

Count me among that group.

"We're a millennial couple and like many in our cohort, student loans are a scary line item on our marital budget." [2] Erin is an author and personal finance blogger who has written "Broke Millennial: Takes On Investing" and "Broke Millennial: Stop Scraping By and Get Your Financial Life

Together." She even asked the question in her article, "What kind of a personal finance author would I be if we went on a fancy honeymoon instead of paying off the remainder of my husband's student debt?"[4]

Exactly.

She continued, "So much of prevailing rhetoric in the personal finance industry demonizes all forms of debt and has turned it into a morality issue. But there's a fundamental problem with telling people to eschew all of life's luxuries (big or small) in the quest to be debt-free. 'Because crash diets end at the buffet line,' says H. Jude Boudreaux, CFP, partner and senior financial planner at The Planning Center. He thinks the black-and-white argument of denying yourself breaks while paying off debt is a false choice."[5]

Let me get this straight: Diets don't work, so why even try? You're gonna' end up at the buffet line. Self-denial is a bad thing and paying off debt is a "false choice"?

No wonder our world is in the mess we're in.

Ms. Lowry said, "When I looked at our savings and goals, the numbers told me to ditch the honeymoon and become debt-free. My emotions said otherwise."[5]

Of course they did. The Bible says, "The heart is deceitful above all things, and desperately sick; who can understand it?" (Jeremiah 17:9). She ended the article by saying she could sleep well at night knowing the extra eight months' interest that would accrue because they went on the honeymoon instead of paying off their debt was "money well spent: It's a down payment on a strong foundation for our marriage."[6]

What?

This is personal to me. For too many years I followed the advice of the wrong people. So many who echoed the same philosophy as the article above. We went on vacations we couldn't afford, charged them to our credit card and spent the next 10 months to a year – every year – paying them off so we could do it all over again. Went out to eat when we couldn't really afford it. Spent money buying things we really didn't need, so we could fit in with our friends. The sad reality was they were in the same debt pit we were in, but no one admitted it.

When we first got married, I was buying a new car almost every six months until I couldn't do it anymore because we couldn't afford it. We lived miserly and miserably for years until I decided to change and thankfully, my family went along with me.

For too many years I followed the advice of the wrong people.

Overnight we went from self-indulgence to self-denial; from a debt-based life to a cash-based life. If we didn't have the money for something, anything, we didn't need it and we weren't getting it. Yes, it was horrible not doing whatever we wanted to do while everyone else was. But we had a plan and we'd established priorities we weren't going to bend on. Like putting God first, denying every urge to splurge, disciplining ourselves to live frugally and sensibly. Which meant paying off all our debts and changing the way we'd managed whatever God gave us.

Today we can do whatever we want, whenever we want; go wherever we want, help whoever we want, and get whatever we need. We pay cash for everything and have committed ourselves to helping as many people as we can to enjoy the same kind of life we've been enjoying for almost 20 years.

So, what is the plan we follow? It's pretty simple. You can sum it up in four words: **Pay now, play later.** It's not as much fun at first, but the benefits will last until the day you die.

What are you waiting on?

---

1 Lowry, Erin. "Millennials: Go Ahead and Take That Vacation Instead of Paying off Your Student Debt." USA Today, Gannett Satellite Information Network, www.usatoday.com/story/money/columnist/2019/09/26/millennials-need-take-honeymoon-then-finish-paying-off-debt/2421112001/.

2 IBID

3 IBID

4 IBID

5 IBID

6 IBID

GIVING: TITHES & OFFERINGS

By Barry Cameron, September 13, 2019

There's no argument when it comes to giving to God. It all belongs to Him – ALL OF IT – period (Psalm 24:1). When King David and all his people had given so willingly, generously and sacrificially to build God's temple, he said to God, "Who am I, and what is my people that we should be able thus to offer willingly? For all things come from you, and of your own have we given you" (1 Chronicles 29:14). David knew what most people today still don't get: we never give God anything of ours. Everything we have came from Him.

Mark Batterson, in his excellent book **ALL IN**, writes: "I cannot prove this quantitatively, but I know it's true: the more you give away, the more you will enjoy what you have. If you give God the tithe, you'll enjoy the 90 percent you keep 10 percent more. You'll also discover that God can do more with 90 percent than you can do with 100 percent … Most of us spend most of our lives accumulating the wrong things. We've bought into the consumerist lie that more is more. But in God's upside-down economy, our logic is backward. You ultimately lose whatever you keep and you ultimately keep whatever you lose for the cause of Christ."

Jack Graham, Pastor of the great Prestonwood Baptist Church in Plano, said, "The purpose of tithing is to teach us to put God first in our lives. God doesn't need our money. Instead, He wants what our money represents: our priorities, passions, purposes. Make a commitment to tithe and dedicate yourself to it. And more than anything … trust God and let Him prove His promises."

Tithing is giving back to God 10 percent of whatever He blesses us with financially. God said, "Bring the whole tithe into the storehouse, that there may be food in my house. 'Test me in this,' says the Lord Almighty, 'and see if I will not throw open the floodgates of heaven and pour out so much blessing that you will not have room enough for it'" (Malachi 3:10/ NIV1984).

Dr. Charles Stanley says the storehouse generally meant "His tabernacle or temple in the Old Testament, and the church in the New Testament. We are to give our tithes wherever we regularly worship the Lord – not only to care for the church building and those who work there but to support the expansion of His kingdom by spreading the gospel and ministering to the community for His name's sake."

Tithing is not the finish line in giving; it's the starting line. Every Christian ought to at least be a faithful tither of everything God gives them. It's hard to "run the race" that has been set before you (Hebrews 12:1) if you haven't begun to trust God with your finances. Why is it so easy for us to trust God to save us, but when it comes to trusting Him with our money (more accurately, the money He has given us), we struggle? Especially when He's told us to bring the whole tithe and "test Him" to see if He won't "open the floodgates of Heaven and pour out so much blessing" that we won't have room enough for it.

You may have heard arguments **AGAINST** tithing. Here are six arguments FOR tithing:

(1) **The LOGICAL argument.**

Consider the logic. In Matthew 5:27-28, Jesus said, "You have heard that it was said, 'You shall not commit adultery.' But I say to you that everyone who looks at a woman with lustful intent has already committed adultery with her in his heart." **Jesus raised the standard to a higher level than before.**

In Matthew 5:21-22, Jesus said, "You have heard that it was said to those of old, 'You shall not murder; and whoever murders will be liable to judgment.' But I say to you that everyone who is angry with his brother will be liable to judgment." **Once again, Jesus raised the standard to a higher level than before.**

Over and over again, in the Sermon on the Mount, Jesus said, "You have heard it said, but I say to you," and **He raised everything to a higher level than before.** So what would make someone think when it comes to tithing, Jesus would now say, "I understand about the tithe, giving 10 percent back to God in the Old Testament. But here's how it works now: you just decide whatever you want to give and whatever you want to give is fine with Me."

Some will quote 2 Corinthians 9:7 where Paul said, "Each one must give as he has decided in his heart, not reluctantly or under compulsion, for God loves a cheerful giver," as their response. However, the context of that verse is an over and above love offering for the poor saints in Jerusalem. In the case of love offerings above and beyond the tithe, each one should decide in his own heart, and we should give cheerfully and generously as we are able.

(2) **The CUSTODIAL argument.**

Whose money is this anyway? The fact is we brought nothing into this world and won't be taking anything out of this world (Job 1:21). We're just privileged custodians, and we're supposed to be faithful stewards (1 Corinthians 4:2) of whatever blessings God gives us for a few years here on earth. He gives them, and He can take them away (Haggai 1:5-11). Because He's God and everything belongs to Him and everything we have comes from Him, we're to honor Him with the "firstfruits of all our produce (income)" (Proverbs 3:9-10).

Even when we are faithful tithers (giving 10 percent of our income back to God), we need to keep in mind the 90 percent left over is STILL HIS. We're just managers, stewards, custodians.

(3) The BIBLICAL argument.

Tithing is a Bible doctrine not just an Old Testament teaching (Malachi 3:8-12; Leviticus 27:30; Deuteronomy 12:11; Proverbs 3:9-10). It's in the New Testament, which comes as a surprise to many. Especially to those who don't tithe and have used that erroneous claim as an excuse not to do so. We have two reliable eyewitness accounts in Matthew 23:23 and Luke 11:42 where Jesus affirmed and encouraged the practice of tithing. In Luke 18:12, Jesus used the example of tithing in telling a parable to illustrate the folly of self-righteousness. If tithing were only for the Old Testament Israelites and had no bearing whatsoever on, or importance to, anyone living during New Testament times or beyond, why would Jesus use it as an illustration when He's communicating biblical truths?

Tithing is also mentioned in Hebrews 7:1-10 no less than **seven times**. It recounts how Abraham gave tithes (or a tenth) to Melchizedek the king/priest. The point of the passage is that Jesus is better than Melchizedek and His priesthood is far superior to that of Melchizedek's.

By the way, Abraham tithed long before the law was ever established; so did Jacob. In Genesis 28, after Jacob had an incredible dream about how God was going to bless him and use him, he set up a memorial stone and made a commitment "of all that you give me I will give a full tenth to you" (Genesis 28:22).

(4) The CHRISTOLOGICAL argument.

What did Jesus say about tithing?

Matthew 23:23, "Woe to you, scribes and Pharisees, hypocrites!

For you tithe mint and dill and cumin, and have neglected the weightier matters of the law: justice and mercy and faithfulness. These you ought to have done, without neglecting the others."

Luke 11:42, "But woe to you Pharisees! For you tithe mint and rue and every herb, and neglect justice and the love of God. These you ought to have done, without neglecting the others."

If tithing were irrelevant or unnecessary, wouldn't Jesus have said, "Why are you still tithing? You don't have to do that anymore." Instead, when referencing tithing, He said, "These you ought to have to done."

Tithing is also clearly implied in what Jesus said in Matthew 22:21, "Therefore render (or give) to Caesar the things that are Caesar's, and to God the things that are God's." How would they know what was Caesar's? Simple, Caesar told them. Just like Uncle Sam does today and it is always a percentage of our income.

(5) The TEMPORAL argument.

Think about this ... we give at least 15 percent, more likely 18-20 percent, to "temporary servants" for "temporary meals" in a "temporary world." So why would we give less than that to The Eternal God of the universe Who has given us eternal life and blessings, which, if we were honest, would take us an eternity just to list them all?

(6) The FINAL argument.

In the final analysis, what are you going to be glad you did once you step out into eternity? Some people excuse the fact they don't tithe by saying they tithe in other ways. The Bible says, "A tithe of everything belongs to the Lord and is holy to the Lord" (Leviticus 27:30). We should tithe our time and our talents, etc. But we are also to tithe our treasure (Proverbs 3:9-10; Malachi 3:8-12; Matthew 22:21).

Do you want to stand before God and explain why you looked

175

for every opportunity and rationalization you could find to get out of giving what was rightfully His?

Do you want to have to answer why you gave yourself the best and gave Him leftovers? If there was anything left over? Even though Jesus said, "Seek first the kingdom of God and His righteousness, and all these things will be added to you" (Matthew 6:33).

Or do you want to hear God say, "Well done, good and faithful servant"?

Luke 21:1-4 says one day Jesus was watching what people gave as they put their gifts in the offering box. He noticed several rich people putting their gifts in and Luke says, "He saw a poor widow put in two small copper coins. And he said, 'Truly, I tell you, this poor widow has put in more than all of them. For they all contributed out of their abundance, but she out of her poverty put in all she had to live on.'"

Jesus' point was: out of her pittance came abundance. But out of their abundance came pittance. We can't say our heart is right until our treasure is right.

… And it all begins with the tithe.

Jesus said, "For where your treasure is, there will your heart will be also" (Matthew 6:21).

THE POINT OF NO RETURN

By Barry Cameron, April 17, 2019

"Your pastor is dead," the leader said. "The man who loved you enough to tell you about JESUS, giving you the opportunity of eternal life, has been killed because of his faith. This is the cost of following JESUS." [1]

Those words, spoken by a church leader in Iran, would be unnerving in any setting. However, it was especially chilling because he was addressing 38 men and women from a Muslim background who had come to be baptized. How would they respond now? And who would blame them if they had second thoughts and decided to wait and pray some more about it?

Nik Ripken, a leading expert on the persecuted church with personal experience and research in over seventy countries, shared this story in an article for Christianity Today (April 13, 2019). He said, "Within Islamic settings, Muslims equate baptism with salvation. Seekers from Islam investigating a relationship with Jesus Christ can explain away many of their activities.

"If they're discovered reading the Bible, they can claim they are studying it in order to debate Christians more intelligently. If they're seen sneaking into a church building, they can excuse such behavior in the same way. If seen talking to a pastor or some Western Christian, seekers can suggest that they were simply observed witnessing, lifting up the attributes of Islam.

"But they can't explain away baptism – there is no acceptable excuse.

"Muslims believe that at baptism, a person no longer belongs to Islam but to Christianity. They have left one community and joined another. The local community says that when converts are baptized, they have left Muhammad and joined with Jesus. At baptism, persecution soars because identification with Jesus is real, irrevocable, and forever.

"Baptism is the point of no return." [2]

Most people in America have little or no idea of the persecution believers face in other parts of the world because we haven't come close to reaching the point of being threatened or killed for our faith. And stories like this one don't really shake us like they should.

At baptism, identification with Jesus is real, irrevocable and forever!

Even more concerning is the view many hold of baptism, as if it's an option we can choose or skip if we want. Millions read Bibles, attend church services, hang out with Christians, but that doesn't mean they're *ALL IN.* According to Nik Ripken that doesn't even garner much attention from the Muslims. But if you decide to be baptized, that's a different story. Because baptism is the point of no return.

Baptism is the clear command from Christ (Matthew 28:19; Acts 10:48), passionately preached and practiced by the early church (Acts 2:38-41; 8:36-38; 9:18; 16:25-33) perfectly picturing the death, burial and resurrection of our Lord (Romans 6:3-4).

Baptism is the point of no return. Even Muslims know that's when someone is *ALL IN.* To paraphrase Mr. Ripken, at baptism, identification with Jesus is real, irrevocable and forever!

Those 38 believers in Iran "lined up and down the aisle of the church awaiting baptism, were told, 'Your pastor has been killed. Now that you know the cost, are you ready to follow Jesus through baptism and beyond?'

Not one person walked away." [3]

Will you?

1 Ripken, Nik. "Baptism: The Point of No Return." The Exchange | A Blog by Ed Stetzer, www. christianitytoday.com/edstetzer/2019/april/baptism-point-of-no-return-story-somalia-persecution.html.
2 IBID
3 IBID

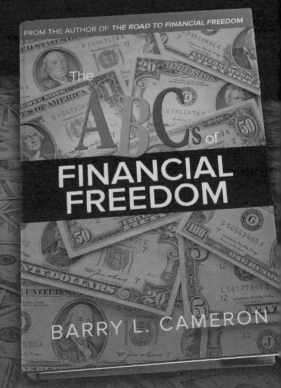

THE KEY TO CONTINUOUS BLESSING!

Generosity is always contagious! It's also supposed to be our normal way of life.

"Every movement has its passionate spokesman: Bill Bright for discipleship; Rick Warren for purpose-driven living; Ed Young for communicating creatively. Barry Cameron is the spokesman for contagious generosity."

"Get ready to be surprised, challenged, and inspired. Practicing these principles will not only change your life, but change the world for the better."

FROM THE AUTHOR OF *THE ABCs OF FINANCIAL FREEDOM* AND *THE ROAD TO FINANCIAL FREEDOM*

CONTAGIOUS GENEROSITY
THE KEY TO CONTINUOUS BLESSING!

BARRY L. CAMERON
FOREWORD BY DAVE STONE

AVAILABLE AT

Amazon
or
The Disciple Shop Bookstore
(888) 360-7648